AGENTS AND THEIR ACTIONS

T0373312

Ratio Book Series

Each book in the series is devoted to a philosophical topic of particular contemporary interest, and features invited contributions from leading authorities in the chosen field.

Volumes published so far:

Agents and Their Actions, edited by Maximilian de Gaynesford
Philosophy of Literature, edited by Severin Schroeder
Essays on Derek Parfit's On What Matters, edited by Jussi Suikkanen and John Cottingham
Justice, Equality and Constructivism, edited by Brian Feltham
Wittgenstein and Reason, edited by John Preston
The Meaning of Theism, edited by John Cottingham
Metaphysics in Science, edited by Alice Drewery
The Self?, edited by Galen Strawson
On What We Owe to Each Other, edited by Philip Stratton-Lake
The Philosophy of Body, edited by Mike Proudfoot
Meaning and Representation, edited by Emma Borg
Arguing with Derrida, edited by Simon Glendinning
Normativity, edited by Jonathan Dancy

AGENTS AND THEIR ACTIONS

Edited by

MAXIMILIAN DE GAYNESFORD

WILEY-BLACKWELL

A John Wiley & Sons, Ltd., Publication

This edition first published 2011
Originally published as Volume 23, No. 4 of *Ratio*
Chapters © 2011 The Authors
Book compilation © 2011 Blackwell Publishing Ltd

Blackwell Publishing was acquired by John Wiley & Sons in February 2007. Blackwell's publishing program has been merged with Wiley's global Scientific, Technical, and Medical business to form Wiley-Blackwell.

Registered Office
John Wiley & Sons Ltd, The Atrium, Southern Gate, Chichester, West Sussex, PO19 8SQ, United Kingdom

Editorial Offices
350 Main Street, Malden, MA 02148-5020, USA
9600 Garsington Road, Oxford, OX4 2DQ, UK
The Atrium, Southern Gate, Chichester, West Sussex, PO19 8SQ, UK

For details of our global editorial offices, for customer services, and for information about how to apply for permission to reuse the copyright material in this book please see our website at www.wiley.com/wiley-blackwell.

The right of Maximilian de Gaynesford to be identified as the author of the editorial material in this work has been asserted in accordance with the Copyright, Designs and Patents Act 1988.

Wiley also publishes its books in a variety of electronic formats. Some content that appears in print may not be available in electronic books.

Designations used by companies to distinguish their products are often claimed as trademarks. All brand names and product names used in this book are trade names, service marks, trademarks or registered trademarks of their respective owners. The publisher is not associated with any product or vendor mentioned in this book. This publication is designed to provide accurate and authoritative information in regard to the subject matter covered. It is sold on the understanding that the publisher is not engaged in rendering professional services. If professional advice or other expert assistance is required, the services of a competent professional should be sought.

Library of Congress Cataloging-in-Publication Data

Agents and their actions / edited by Maximilian de Gaynesford.
     p.   cm. – (Ratio special issues)
  Includes bibliographical references and index.
  ISBN 978-1-4443-3908-6 (pbk.)
  1. Act (Philosophy)   2. Agent (Philosophy)   I. De Gaynesford, Maximilian.
  B105.A35A46 2011
  128'.4–dc22
                                        2011015193

This book is published in the following electronic formats: ePDFs (9781444346732); Wiley Online Library (9781444346763); ePub (9781444346749); Kindle (9781444346756)

Set in 11/12 pt New Baskerville by Toppan Best-set Premedia Limited
Printed in Malaysia by Ho Printing (M) Sdn Bhd

1   2011

CONTENTS

NOTES ON CONTRIBUTORS

Maria Alvarez is Senior Lecturer at King's College London.

Maximilian de Gaynesford is Professor at the University of Reading.

Laura W. Ekstrom is Associate Professor at the College of William and Mary.

John Hyman is Professor at the University of Oxford.

John McDowell is Distinguished University Professor at the University of Piitsburgh.

Joseph Raz is Professor at Columbia University Law School.

Robert Stern is Professor at the University of Sheffield.

PREFACE

Contemporary Philosophy of Action is like Plutarch's Mediterranean: a well-mixed bowl. It is here that much of the most interesting recent work in metaphysics and epistemology is blended with compelling new material in ethics, logic and the philosophy of mind and language. This collection reflects the phenomenon, which is full of promise for the future. The ingredients are gathered from every major area of philosophy, but they merge in efforts to understand action and agency.

John McDowell extends his path-breaking account of intentionality in *Mind and World* by exploring the implications for intention in action. Joseph Raz develops his influential views about rational agency with an analysis of responsibility. Laura Ekstrom shows how a self that is capable of acting wholeheartedly depends on structures that combine preferences with convictions. John Hyman deepens his account of the way knowledge works by examining its uses and roles in guiding action. Robert Stern demonstrates how historical debate may elucidate current controversy, comparing Korsgaard with Kant on the nature of agency. Maria Alvarez uses action and agency to understand premises and conclusions, the elements of practical reasoning. The final chapter uses action to distinguish various types of utterance.

John Cottingham has been most generous with help and advice in putting this collection together. My fellow-contributors have been patient and accommodating. I am grateful to them all. The book is dedicated to my daughter Elisabeth, whose agency is as puzzling as anyone's, but whose actions are a day-long delight.

Maximilian de Gaynesford
April 2011

1

REASONS FOR ACTION AND PRACTICAL REASONING

Maria Alvarez

Abstract
This chapter seeks a better understanding of the elements of practical reasoning: premises and conclusion. It argues that the premises of practical reasoning do not normally include statements such as 'I want to φ'; that the reasoning in practical reasoning is the same as in theoretical reasoning and that what makes it *practical* is, first, that the point of the relevant reasoning is given by the goal that the reasoner seeks to realize by means of that reasoning and the subsequent action; second, that the premises of such reasoning show the goodness of the action to be undertaken; third, that the conclusions of such reasoning may be actions or decisions, that can be accompanied by expressions of intention, either *in* action, or for the future; and that these are justified, and might be contradicted, in ways that are not only peculiar to them (i.e. in ways that diverge from those found in theoretical reasoning), but are distinctively practical, in that they involve reference to reasons for *acting* and to expressions of *intention*, respectively.[1]

This chapter explores practical reasoning. In particular, it seeks a better understanding of the elements of practical reasoning (premises and conclusion) and their relation. These are large and much debated issues. I shall first focus on the question: 'What are the premises of practical reasoning?' and, towards the end of the chapter, will say something about the conclusion of practical reasoning. As will become clear, my discussion is inspired in Elizabeth Anscombe's remarks on practical reasoning in *Intention* and in her paper 'Practical Inference'.[2]

[1] I should like to thank John Broome, Alex Neill, Aaron Ridley, Daniel Whiting and participants at seminars where earlier versions of this chapter were presented for their comments and suggestions.

[2] G.E.M. Anscombe, *Intention* (Oxford: Blackwell, 1957); and 'Practical Inference', in *Human Life, Action and Ethics*, ed. M. Geach and L. Gormally (Exeter: Imprint Academic, 2005), pp. 109–48. For a detailed discussion of Anscombe's views on this see, C. Vogler, 'Anscombe on Practical Inference' in E. Millgram, ed., *Varieties of Practical Reasoning* (MIT University Press, 2001), pp. 437–64.

2   MARIA ALVAREZ

A preliminary point. The term 'practical reasoning', one might think, is ambiguous, for it can be used to refer to the process of practical reasoning, or to the 'content' of that reasoning. I am not convinced by this ambiguity claim. At any rate, by 'practical reasoning' I shall here mean the reasoning that we, as rational agents, engage in. Engaging in such reasoning is taking certain statements as premises and, if all goes well, reaching a 'practical' conclusion, which has those premises as its grounds. So the questions I am concerned with can be put without ambiguity: what kind of statements play the role of premises when we engage in practical reasoning? And what is the conclusion of such reasoning?

The premises of practical reasoning

Many contemporary philosophers think the following gives the form of the most basic and simple piece of practical reasoning:

P1. I want to φ
P2. I believe that ψ-ing is a means of φ-ing
C. I shall/ should / ought to/ must, ψ.[3]

That is, for many contemporary philosophers, the *first* premise in practical reasoning is a statement such as 'I want to φ'.[4]

It is, then, striking, though not surprising, that one should find the following remark in Anscombe's discussion of practical reasoning: ' "I want" does not rightly occur in the premises [of practical reasoning]'.[5]

---

[3] The first premise is sometimes said to be: 'I intend to φ'; and the conclusion is sometimes given as: 'I intend to ψ'. For my purposes here, this difference is of no relevance, so I shall focus on the first suggestion. I shall, however, say something below about versions of practical reasoning that take the first premise and the conclusion to be the 'content' of an intention.

[4] See, e.g. David Velleman, *The Possibility of Practical Reasoning* (Oxford: Oxford University Press, 2000), esp. 193–99, although his account of the sense in which 'I want to φ' is the first premise of practical reason is complex. For a (sympathetic) explanation of this as the basic schema for practical reasoning see also Robert Audi, *Practical Reasoning and Ethical Decision* (London and New York: Routledge, 2006), pp. 96ff. Audi also provides a very helpful survey of various views on the basic structure of practical reasoning on pp. 82–6.

[5] *Intention*, p.ix. The remark appears in the 'Table of Contents' and is developed further in section §35.

I say it is not surprising to find that her view on this is at odds with prevailing contemporary views because she tended to think that contemporary philosophers had lost sight of some important insights about human agency that Aristotle and his medieval commentators had gained. Nonetheless, her remark above requires explanation and defence, for contemporary philosophers certainly have on their side the strong *prima facie* plausibility of the claim that what was given above captures in schematic form how we often summarise the reasoning behind, or leading to, an action.

So why does Anscombe say that 'I want' does not rightly occur in the premises of practical reasoning? In order to answer this question, I shall make explicit something I take to be an uncontroversial claim, namely that whenever an action has a piece of practical reasoning as its grounds, the premises of the relevant practical reasoning are one's reason for acting. Therefore, if we establish what our reasons for acting are, we shall know what kind of statements play the role of premises in practical reasoning, and will then be able to decide whether statements such as 'I want to φ' have any business playing that role. If, having done that, we find that Anscombe is right, then we will still have a question left: what role, if any, do such statements play in practical reasoning?

A point of terminological clarification is needed. The phrase 'one's reasons for acting' may be used refer to the reasons that there are for one to act: what in the literature are called 'normative reasons'. Here, I use the phrase rather to refer to what in the same literature are labelled 'motivating reasons': the reasons for which one acts, when one acts for a reason. These are reasons that favour one's action in one's eyes; they present the action as good or valuable in some respect; and they are the reasons in the light of which one acts.

The view about practical reasoning that I attributed to many contemporary philosophers goes hand in hand with what is often called the 'Humean view of motivating reasons'.[6] This is the view that my reason for ψ-ing is that I want to φ and that I believe that

---

[6] The view is associated with Donald Davidson because of his account of the 'primary reason' why someone acted. See D. Davidson, *Essays on Actions and Events* (Oxford: Oxford University Press, 1980), p. 4. Whether he actually held this view about practical reasoning is not to the point here as it is held by many people who take themselves to be following him on this.

ψ-ing is a means of φ-ing.[7] On this Humean view, then, when someone digs in order to find some treasure his reason for digging is that he wants to find some treasure and believes that digging is the way to find it.[8]

Thus, on this view an agent's reason for ψ-ing, that is, the reasons that motivate him to ψ are that he wants to φ and that he believes that ψ-ing is a means of φ-ing. And since the reason that motivates can play the role of premises in practical reasoning, then, on this view, the premises of practical reasoning are statements to the effect that one wants and believes certain things; in our example, the relevant premises would be 'I want to find some treasure' and 'I believe that digging is the way to find it'.

I have argued elsewhere that this view of motivating reasons is wrong: the reasons that motivate me to act are not, or not typically, that I want something, or that I believe something about how to achieve what I want.[9] But it should be noted that, although both claims are wrong, the claim about wanting is doubly wrong. For, although the fact that I believe something is not normally my reason for acting, *what* I believe can be. So, for example, if I move house because my current house is too small to keep my books in, then my reason for moving house is not that I believe that my current house is too small to keep my books in. However, my reason *is* something I believe (or know): namely, that my current house is too small to keep my books in. By contrast, neither the fact that I want something, nor what I want, is normally my reason for acting.

Here I shall summarise an argument against the idea that the fact that I want something is my reason for acting.[10] Reasons for doing something are, as we saw, reasons that favour the action in the agent's eyes: such reasons encapsulate some feature or property of the prospective action that makes, or appears to the agent to make, the action good or valuable. But, in general, the mere

---

[7]   The idea that doing one thing is a means of doing another is to be interpreted here quite loosely so that doing the one thing may be a way or even an instance of doing the other.

[8]   This view is often thought to imply that motivating reasons are mental states of the agent's but I shall not assess that claim here. See Alvarez, *Kinds of Reasons* (Oxford: Oxford University Press, 2010), chapters 2 and 5.

[9]   See Alvarez, *Kinds of Reasons*, especially chapter 5. I say 'typically' above because they may. I return to this point below.

[10]   I have argued for this in detail elsewhere: see my 'Reasons, Desires and Intentional Actions', in *New Essays on the Explanation of Action*, ed. C. Sandis (London: Plagrave Macmillan, 2008), pp. 203–19; and *Kinds of Reasons*, chapters 3 and 4.

fact that I want to do something does not favour, nor does it appear to me to favour, doing it.

The fact that I want to do something does have a connection with my reason for doing it, but the connection is not that the fact that I want to do it is itself my reason for doing it. Rather, the connection lies in the truth that many of the things we want, we want for reasons. Borrowing a term from Anscombe, we might call my reason for wanting to do something the 'desirability characterisation' that doing it has for me. And that desirability characterisation relates my doing that thing to the good (broadly conceived), because the things we want, we want because we see some good in them (the good may be aesthetic, prudential, hedonic, etc.). Whatever good we see in what we want is the reason why we want that thing; and for many of these things wanted, this good we see in them is also *our* reason for wanting them. As the Aristotelian-mediaeval slogan has it, what is wanted is wanted *sub ratione boni* ('under the aspect of the good').[11] Anscombe puts this point by saying that 'good is the object of wanting' as 'truth is the object of judgment' (*Intention*, p. 77); and she adds:

> it does not follow from this that everything judged must be true, or that everything wanted must be good [. . .] the notion of 'good' that has to be introduced in an account of wanting is not that of what is really good but of what the agent conceives to be good (*Ibid.*).

In this she is following Aristotle, who says that the object of desire 'may be either the real or the apparent good'.[12]

This connection between wanting and the good applies to wanting to do things; and the desirability characterisation that the action has for the agent may be that she sees her doing that thing as good intrinsically or instrumentally. When it is regarded as intrinsically good (and hence it is intrinsically desired), the characterisation refers to something that is a form of the good of human beings, and recognisably so: such as health, or pleasure, or

---

[11] Aquinas's *Summa Theologiae*, T. Gilby (ed.) (Oxford: Blackfriars, 1960–73), 1a2ae, 8, 1. See also Aristotle's *Physics*, II, 3, 195a26; and *Nicomachean Ethics*, 1094a3. All references to Aristotle from *The Complete Works of Aristotle. The Revised Oxford Translation*, J. Barnes, ed. (Princeton, N.J.: Princeton University Press, 1984).

[12] *De Anima* III, 433a28.

friendship, or beauty, etc. In such a case, the agent's answer to what her reason for wanting to do that thing is will be a desirability characterisation that puts an end to the question: 'What for?' (See Anscombe, *Intention*, p. 74). When, by contrast, the desirability characterisation is instrumental, then it is possible to ask the question 'What for?' repeatedly, until we reach an answer that points to an intrinsic good and puts an end to that question.

Although every action that has a piece of practical reasoning as its grounds is done for a reason, the converse does not hold. What is the difference between actions done for a reason that have a piece of practical reasoning as their grounds, and those that are merely done for a reason?

One difference, emphasised by Aristotle, Aquinas and Anscombe, is that the former involve means-end *calculation*.[13] So, for instance, 'Skiing is healthy and fun so I'll go skiing' is not an instance of practical reasoning because no calculation about means to an end is involved here. If I go skiing on the grounds given in that statement, then my reason for going skiing is that it is healthy and fun. But that reason is not a premise in practical reasoning for I engaged in none (not even implicitly) when deciding to go skiing. Consider, by contrast, the following: 'My doctor has recommended relaxing activities to lower my blood pressure; skiing is something I find relaxing, so I'll go skiing'. Here, there is calculation about how to achieve an end (lowering my blood pressure through relaxation) and there is therefore practical reasoning. And the premises in this reasoning are my reasons for going skiing: that my doctor has recommended relaxing activities; that skiing is something I find relaxing, etc. It is possible, though not necessary, that there should have been more premises in between the first premise and the conclusion; for instance, premises comparing the relative merits of skiing with other relaxing activities vis-à-vis the end in view; and perhaps vis-à-vis other ends I have. For instance: 'Sailing is also relaxing; but it'll be harder to find sailing companions than skiing companions. Besides sailing is more dangerous/ expensive/ etc., than skiing and is not such good exercise'. And so on. Each of these statements are premises in my reasoning and are also my reasons for going skiing, if that is what I do on the grounds of this reasoning. The premises together show what the good of going skiing is for me; in

13   See Aristotle, Aquinas, 1a, q.22, a.1 ad.3 (*et passim*); Anscombe, *Intention*, pp. 60ff.

this case, that it is a relatively inexpensive and healthy way of achieving my end.

Practical reasoning is employed, according to this view, in order to find means to achieving an end the agent has already settled upon, or to determine which end to pursue among various ends one has. Some of the ends that practical reasoning is deployed to achieve may themselves be the result of practical reasoning, namely those ends that are viewed by the agent as themselves instrumental to other ends. But ultimately each piece of practical reasoning will be related to some end that is itself not the result of the calculation of practical reasoning. Those are the ends that put an end to the question: 'What for?' for they are ends that are instances of some form of the good of human beings.[14]

So, among the reasons that play the role of premises in practical reasoning, some describe what is wanted by reference to some good-making aspect that the wanted thing might have for the agent; for example: 'Skiing is relaxing'; 'It is an exhibition of my favourite artist', etc. Other premises concern facts about different ways of achieving the thing wanted and the relative merits of those different ways of doing so. Examples of these are: 'If I call the ticket office, I can get tickets', 'If we take the train, we'll get to the skiing resort faster than if we drive', 'If I go to the market, I can buy quality trainers at discount prices', etc. (These premises can but need not appear in conditional form; so the same role as above can be played by the corresponding premises: 'one can buy tickets by calling the ticket office', 'taking the train is faster than driving'; 'they sell quality trainers at discount prices at the market'; etc., which give reasons for calling the ticket office, taking the train and going to the market respectively.) Yet other premises in practical reasoning provide background information which, together with premises of the above kind, show why the action is good in the agent's eyes. These premises are very varied: they may state the fact that one lacks a certain good, that circumstances threaten a good one has, or that a good one wants is incompatible with another good one has or wants, etc. Examples of these are: 'The road is flooded', 'It is a fun but very risky

[14] See T. H. Irwin's 'Practical Reason Divided; Aquinas and his Critics', in *Ethics and Practical Deliberation*, G. Cullity and B. Gaut, eds. (Oxford: Clarendon Press, 1997), pp. 189–214, for a discussion of Aquinas's views on the role of practical reasoning concerning 'prudence', which relates to finding means; and to 'synderesis' which relates to the grasp of 'the end aimed at by the moral virtues' (p. 203).

activity'; 'It is raining', 'His illness is very infectious', 'It will be quite expensive', 'We'll miss the movie', 'It is terribly boring', etc. In addition, a piece of practical reasoning may but need not include statements about the relative merits of different ways of achieving a goal and of the impact of doing so on achieving other goals the agent may have: it need not because we do not always reason to the best or even the better means of achieving our goals; often the reasoning seeks simply satisfactory means of doing so.

Thus, the premises of practical reasoning jointly show what good (or apparent good) there is in my doing something. But among those premises we won't normally find the mere fact that I want to do something because that fact does not normally contribute to the good-making characteristics of the action. What does contribute, and what we will find among the premises, is statements that describe the thing wanted and give the agent's reason for wanting to do that thing (and, needless to say, many of these statements may be implicit in one's reasoning.)

Let me turn to the qualification 'normally' that I've just made and was mentioned earlier. I say 'normally' because the fact that I want something might, in unusual cases, occur in the premises of practical reasoning. For instance, I might reason as follows: I want to eat chocolate all the time; but wanting to eat chocolate all the time must be a symptom of some kind of physiological dysfunction, so . . . I'll visit a doctor.[15] Here the fact that I want to eat chocolate all the time is part of my reason for visiting the doctor. So here my want, or more accurately, the fact that I want something is a premise. But that want (to eat chocolate) is not an end that the reasoning is aimed to achieve: that end is rather being healthy. So here the fact that I want to eat chocolate (a premise) plays a very different role from that played by the fact that I want to be healthy.[16]

Thus, if we put aside unusual examples such as the one just examined, where 'I want to φ' is among the premises, we can see why, as Anscombe argued, 'I want to φ' does not rightly occur in the premises of practical reasoning: those premises tell us what the good of the action is, and the fact that I want to do something does not do this, although the fact that what I want to do has some

---

[15]   The same is true of the fact that I believe something. To paraphrase an example of Ryle's, the fact that I cannot help believing that the ice will crack and the fact that my believing this makes me very unsteady on my skates may be my reason for refraining from skating – even though I know that it is very unlikely that the ice will crack.
[16]   See Anscombe's 'Practical Inference', pp. 115–16.

good-making feature (or appears to me to do so) does. This brings us to a question I mentioned in the first section above: if Anscombe is right that 'I want to φ' does not rightly occur in the premises of practical reasoning, what role, if any, do such statements play in practical reasoning? The following passage can help us towards an answer to that question:

> The rôle of 'wanting' in the practical syllogism is quite different from that of a premise. It is that whatever is described in the proposition that is the starting-point of the argument must be wanted in order for the reasoning to lead to any action (Anscombe, *Intention*, p. 66).

Several points can, I think, be derived from this passage – some of which Anscombe makes explicitly elsewhere. I shall focus on the following two:

(i) What is wanted by someone who engages in practical reasoning is, in a sense to be explained, the starting point of practical reasoning.
(ii) What makes reasoning *practical* is that it leads to intentional action.

I shall examine each of these claims, starting with the first.

Practical reasoning and goals

As I said earlier, the claim that 'I want to φ' only very rarely appears as a premise in practical reasoning may strike one as patently false. For we often say, 'I want to φ, ψ-ing is a means of φ-ing, so I'll ψ'. And one might insist that, although this may not be a very sophisticated piece of practical reasoning, it is, contrary to what Anscombe says, an instance of practical reasoning all the same. I have argued that it is not but my claim can be made more acceptable if I can provide an explanation of what arguments of the kind just given (if they are arguments) express.[17]

---

[17] We are inclined to think that they are arguments because the connective 'so' suggests this; but of course that is not a decisive factor. Consider: 'He wanted more money so I told him that he could leave the company'.

I said above that claiming that 'I want to φ' is my reason for
acting is, in a sense, more wrong than saying that 'I believe that p'
is my reason for acting because although neither are (normally)
my reasons, and therefore neither are premises in practical reasoning, what I believe can be, whereas what I want cannot be.[18]
And this is because what I want is not a reason but a goal.[19]

Thus, what is wanted, though not a reason, does play a central
role in practical reasoning and in action – it is that for the sake of
which we reason and act. As Aristotle put it, *to orekton*, what is
wanted, is the starting point of motivation and of practical reasoning. Thus, he asks what is the source of (local) movement for us,
and he answers:

> Both of these then are capable of originating local movement,
> thought and appetite; thought, that is, which calculates means
> to an end, i.e. practical thought (it differs from speculative
> thought in the character of its end); while appetite is in every
> form of it relative to an end; for *that which is the object of appetite
> is the stimulant of practical thought.*[20]

So, according to Aristotle, on the one hand there are goals, which
are 'the objects of appetite' and 'the stimulant of practical
thought'. On the other hand, there is practical thought, which
involves means-ends reasoning about how to achieve those goals,
as well as about how the satisfaction of one goal may affect other
goals one also has, etc.[21]

A goal is something wanted and as such, as we saw earlier, it can
be wanted for its own sake, or as a means to something else. If the
goal is wanted for its own sake – because it is regarded as a good
in itself – then the practical reasoning stands on its own, as it were,

---

[18] Unlike what I believe, what I want (or intend, etc.) does not even have the right form
to be a reason because it is not propositional in form; what I want is, e.g. to buy a new
house, to excel at bridge, to get a more balanced view of this issue, etc., and even when
these are expressed as 'that'-clauses, the corresponding clauses do not express propositions, at least not without doing some violence to the grammar of the relevant language. I
discuss this further in my *Kinds of Reasons*, chapter 3. But see Broome, 'Practical Reasoning', in *Reason and Nature: Essays in the Theory of Rationality*, ed. J. Bermudez and A. Millar
(Oxford: Oxford University Press, 2002), pp. 85–112; p. 87 for the contrary view about the
content of intentions.
[19] Of course, wants are sometimes called 'reasons' but my point is that, even so, they are
not premises in reasoning.
[20] *De Anima*, Book III, section 10; 433a, 14–18. My italics.
[21] On this see also Aquinas, *Summa Theologiae*, 1a2ae, q.1.

i.e., without needing to be underwritten by a reason for pursuing that goal. Thus, if my goal is skiing then the first premise might be 'Skiing is healthy and fun', which describes what is wanted (skiing) under the aspect that makes it good for the agent (health and enjoyment), so the question: why have this goal? does not arise. When the goal is something wanted instrumentally, then we can question the value or goodness of the goal (for example, we may question why someone should want to collect paper clips). This process of questioning the value of one's goal can be repeated until one reaches the specification of a goal that shows that it is something wanted for its own sake, because it is regarded by the agent as something that is intrinsically good. Here, the question: 'Why want that?' does not arise – because, and to the extent that, it is possible to see how, for the agent, that goal embodies some form of the good.

Now we can see that although 'I want to φ, ψ-ing is a means of φ-ing, so I shall ψ' are not statements of the premises and conclusion of a piece of practical reasoning, they do convey information about the relevant practical reasoning. In particular, 'I want to φ' states what the agent who engages in practical reasoning wants. And in stating this we state the *point* of the piece of practical reasoning – which is the goal for the sake of which the agent engages in practical reasoning and for the sake of which he acts, if he acts on that reasoning. Thus, Aquinas says: 'Good has the aspect of an end, and the end is indeed first in the order of intention and last in the order of execution':[22] thus, a goal, which is something wanted under the aspect of the good, is the beginning of practical reasoning (first in the order of intention), and the end of reasoning and action (last in the order of execution). So, although not the first premise, or indeed a premise at all, a goal is the beginning of practical reasoning in the sense that unless an agent has some goal, i.e. something he wants or seeks to achieve, he will not engage in *practical* reasoning (though he may engage in it as an exercise – what Anscombe calls an 'idle practical syllogism').

Thus we see that statements of the kind 'I want to φ' *seem* to be the first premise of practical reasoning because they convey the agent's goal. But, as we have seen, this does not mean that these expressions are premises of practical reasoning, or that they express our reasons for acting. This is, I think, why Anscombe says

that 'it is misleading to put "I want to" into a premise if we are
giving a *formal* account of practical reasoning' (*Intention*, p. 65).
And this brings me to the second point: (ii) What makes reasoning *practical* is that it leads to intentional action.

Practical reasoning

I have argued that the premises of practical reasoning include
statements that describe the agent's goal, including the agent's
reasons for having that goal and others that describe means of
achieving that goal; and added that they may but need not include
statements of the relative merits of different means to achieve that
goal, and of the consequences that taking those means could have
for other things wanted by the agent. To that extent, the premises
of practical reasoning do not seem to differ from those of theoretical reasoning, since both are simply statements of facts. If this is
right, the question arises: what makes practical reasoning *practical?*
One way of approaching this question is by exploring the distinction between theoretical and practical reasoning. However,
although the distinction between them seems intuitive, its precise
nature is hard to capture. It is often said that the distinction lies
in the fact that theoretical reasoning is reasoning about what to
believe, while practical reasoning is reasoning about what to do.
On this view, what distinguishes theoretical and practical reasoning is basically the subject matter of the premises and the
conclusion: in practical reasoning these concern actions.
However, as Anscombe argues, it's plausible to think that the
different is more fundamental:

> I have always objected to accounts of practical reasoning which
> reduce it to theoretical reasoning, i.e. to the argument from the
> truth of the premises to the truth of a conclusion implied by
> them (. . .) My own view is that the conclusion of a practical
> syllogism is an action or decision – that a man draws this con-
> clusion shows that he wants to have or avoid something men-
> tioned in the premises, and that the premises show what the
> point of the decision or action was.[23]

---

[23] G.E.M. Anscombe, 'Commentary on Chisholm's "Practical Reason and the Logic of
Requirement" ', in S. Korner, ed., *Practical Reason* (Oxford: Blackwell, 1974), p. 19.

So this passage provides some features which, according to Anscombe, characterise practical reasoning. The first of the three positive claims she makes concerns the conclusion of practical reasoning, while the last two concern the premises and the purpose (the 'point') of the reasoning.

I have already examined and endorsed the second and third points by arguing that the premises of practical reasoning do not include statements that the agent wants something although they mention or describe what is wanted. I have also argued that practical reasoning presupposes a goal in the person who engages in the reasoning, which is precisely the thing wanted and what gives the *point* of the reasoning and of the action to which the reasoning leads.[24]

Before turning to the much debated question of whether the conclusion of practical reasoning is an action, I want to comment on what this passages says (or implies) about the relation between theoretical and practical reasoning.

In the passage Anscombe warns against reducing practical to theoretical reasoning, in the sense of taking the former to be reasoning from the truth of premises to the truth of a conclusion implied by them. But if practical reasoning is not to be thus reduced to theoretical reasoning, how are the two kinds of reasoning related? One way of conceiving of this relation is the following. Theoretical reasoning is reasoning whose formal object is truth: reasoning from the truth of premises to the truth of a conclusion. Practical reasoning *exploits* theoretical reasoning in the sense that in practical reasoning we put theoretical reasoning to a practical use. We put reasoning to that use when we have a goal – something we want to achieve and indeed something that we believe we can achieve – and reason about how to achieve it. In that respect, as Anscombe says, the subject matter of practical reasoning *is* restricted to 'future matters which our actions can affect' (*Practical Inference*, p. 131): that is, to what can be brought about by one, however indirectly, and hence about what is in the future and what involves one's acting. Moreover, the goal governs the use to which theoretical reasoning is put in two ways: it determines which facts to select as premises, namely, those related to the value of the goal and to the means of achieving it; and it also

---

[24] Unless, that is, one is just reflecting on how practical reasoning works, or reasoning on someone else's behalf, as a detective might when trying to guess how someone might have acted.

determines when to stop reasoning, namely, when we reach (what seems to be) a satisfactory means of achieving the goal (cf. Anscombe, *Practical Inference*, p. 116. There Anscombe shows how the premises of a piece of theoretical reasoning that, for instance, establishes that the contents of a bottle is poisonous to humans might come to en end with the – normally unstated – premise 'I am a human', given a certain goal, e.g. suicide; or it may instead end with 'NN is a human', given a very different goal; e.g. murder.) Thus, the premises of practical reasoning are statements of fact about things we desire and possible means of achieving those things; *which* such statements we attend to, and *when* we stop reasoning, is partly determined by the goals we have and for the sake of which we engage in practical reasoning. But the statements we attend to, and the truth relations between them, are just those of theoretical reasoning:[25]

> The considerations and their logical relations are just the same whether the inference is practical or theoretical. What I mean by the 'considerations' are all those hypotheticals which we have been considering, and also any propositions which show them to be true. The difference between practical and theoretical is mainly a difference in the service to which these considerations are put.[26]

Perhaps this way of understanding the relation between theoretical and practical reasoning is part of what Aristotle means when he says that practical thought 'differs from speculative thought in the character of its end' (*De Anima*, 433a, 15–16), if we understand this to mean that practical thought is theoretical thought put to a practical end.

Let me now turn to the question about the conclusion of practical reasoning – although this is a complex issue to which it won't be possible to do justice here. The view that Anscombe explicitly endorses in the passage quoted at the beginning of this section,

[25] With the qualification about the subject matter of practical reasoning mentioned above.
[26] Anscombe, *Practical Inference*, p. 132. See also pp. 122ff, for her discussion of Kenny's suggestion (developed in his *Will, Freedom and Power* (Oxford: Blackwell, 1975), ch.7) that practical reasoning follows a 'logic of satisfactoriness', which is 'the mirror image of ordinary logic'. This seems to provide an interesting way of construing the idea that practical reasoning exploits theoretical reasoning.

namely that the conclusion of practical reasoning is an action (or a decision – more on this later), is often associated with Aristotle.[27] But the view has seemed unacceptable to many, on various grounds.

Some reject it on the grounds that practical reasoning does not require any physical ability, while action (except for so-called 'mental acts') does, therefore practical reasoning cannot have an action as its conclusion. After all, one may conclude a piece of reasoning, e.g. by deciding that one shall φ, only to find out that one has become paralysed and cannot φ; or only to change one's mind later and decide against it. And here it seems that the relevant practical reasoning has been concluded before any action has been undertaken, so the conclusion of practical reasoning cannot be the action – the action is, we might say, the implementation of the conclusion.[28]

These considerations have some force but not enough, I think, to show that the conclusion of practical reasoning can never be an action. Or to put the point differently, part of their force derives from the fact that practical reasoning often concerns what to do in the future. In those cases, the conclusion may be a decision to act in the future and the subsequent action, if any, will be the implementation of the decision. But in cases where the practical reasoning concerns what to do now, there seems to be less reason to accept that the conclusion may not be an action. For if action is due now, there need not be a prior decision (or an intention) that is separate from the action: in such cases acting is what deciding consists in (and the intention is *in* the action). If so, in such cases the practical reasoning is not complete until the agent acts, for the action *is* the conclusion of that practical reasoning (both in the sense that the action is what the premises lead to and also in the sense that it is supported by them). Moreover, in cases where the action is in the future, the connection between the decision and the relevant action is such that the performance of

---

[27] For a sceptical view that this is right see Audi, *Practical Reasoning*, p. 23ff.

[28] The following passage seems to capture this objection:

Aristotle took practical reasoning to be reasoning that concludes in an action. But an action – at least a physical one – requires more than reasoning ability; it requires physical ability too. Intending to act is as close to acting as reasoning alone can get us, so we should take practical reasoning to be reasoning that concludes in an intention. (J. Broome, 'Practical Reasoning', p. 85.)

For similar arguments see also Audi, *Practical Reasoning*, 89ff.

the action is one of the *criteria* for attributing the decision to the agent. For if an agent claims, to himself or to others, to have decided to φ but in the absence of external obstacles, or of a change of mind, does not φ when the moment comes, then the claim that he *had decided* to φ comes under threat. And if the decision, as opposed to the action, is the alleged conclusion of practical reasoning, then in such cases it is not clear that the reasoning had indeed reached a conclusion, as the objectors claim. In other words: decision and action are not as separable from each other as the objection suggests.[29]

The reasons against accepting that actions can be the conclusions of practical reasoning are often reasons for the view that the conclusion of practical reasoning must be a judgement. For, on this view, reasoning just is moving from the truth of premises to the truth of a conclusion; and even if there is more to practical reasoning than that, as Anscombe claims, there surely cannot be less. And if this is right, the conclusion must be propositional, i.e. a judgement, or something judgement-like. For instance, the conclusion might be something like: 'I ought to do this'; or 'I must do that'.

There are several things to note about this thought. One is that such a conclusion is not practical, for one may indeed conclude this but not go on to decide to or intend to act; nor, of course, to act. Because of this, it is not clear that that would be a piece of *practical* reasoning. Moreover, this 'judgement' which is supposed to be the conclusion of practical reasoning is not, or at least very often is not, 'necessitated' by the premises. Actions are the subject of choice – and the latter is generally guided by reasons (or at least by apparent reasons, as an agent may deliberate and choose on the basis of false premises which express only apparent reasons). Often, there may be more than one acceptable way of achieving one's goal, and then it is up to one which to choose. Geach expresses this point as follows:

> In theoretical reasoning it cannot be equally justifiable to pass from A, B, C, . . . to a conclusion D and to an incompatible conclusion D'. But in practical deliberation D may be a fiat expressing one way of getting our ends, and D' may express another incompatible way: in that case it may be *up to us*

---

[29] The same, *mutatis mutandis*, is true of intentions as conclusions.

whether from A, B, C, . . . we pass on to accepting D as a guide to action, or rather, to accepting D'.[30]

An example of this might be a choice between walking to work and cycling. Someone may consider the following reasons: both walking and cycling are equally economical, they are good forms of exercise, cycling is faster but walking more relaxing, etc. Here, the overall set of reasons makes either right and therefore it leaves room for choice. It is important to note here that doing either will be explained by the reasons there are to do that thing. So suppose that in those circumstances, I choose to walk. My reasons for choosing that, and hence my reasons for walking, will be that walking is a practical, healthy and economical way to get to work and, though slower than cycling, it's still more relaxing, etc. Had I, on the other hand, chosen to cycle, then my reasons for choosing that would be that cycling is a practical, healthy and economical way to get to work and, though less relaxing, it is quicker than walking, etc.[31]

Whichever course of action one chooses, it is supported, as one might put it, by the premises but it is not implied by them, even if we express the conclusion in propositional form: 'I should walk' or 'I should cycle'. Admittedly, sometimes the reasoning will leave little room for choice, because it shows (or appears to) that there is only one means to achieve one's goal. And in those cases it might indeed seem that the conclusion is implied by the premises. But most often this is not so.[32]

In any case, insisting that the reasoning must have such a conclusion, a judgement, seems to actually obscure the distinctive character of practical reasoning, namely that it is *practical*.[33]

---

[30]   P. Geach, *Reason and Argument*, (Oxford: Blackwell, 1976), p. 98.
[31]   There is also choice between incompatible goals. In that case, we may choose which of the goals to satisfy.
[32]   Both von Wright's and Broome's accounts of practical reasoning are devised so that the conclusion is necessitated, in this sense, by the premises. But because of that, they are both restricted in their application because if they work, they work only for reasoning about the necessary means of doing something.
[33]   Thus Audi, for example, says that the view under consideration has the defect, among others, of making practical reasoning a hybrid process of 'what is, intuitively, reasoning and, on the other hand, action based on it' (*Practical Reasoning*, p. 91). But far from seeming a defect of the view, one might think that this captures what is distinctive of *practical* reasoning, which is precisely a 'hybrid process' consisting of purposive action grounded on (theoretical) reasoning.

And, as we saw above, there is a way of understanding what it is for the premises of reasoning to lead to the practical conclusion other than to imply it, namely the premises are grounds for the action in that they show its goodness relative to some goal of the agent's.

This action-as-conclusion, as Anscombe suggests, may be accompanied by statements such as 'I'm φ-ing' in the case where the reasoning results in intentional action 'straightaway'; or 'I shall φ' when the action is in the future. And thus we may think of these as some kind of propositional correlates of the intentional action. But there is something important to notice about these statements, namely that they are *expressions of intention*: the first of intention 'in action', and the second of intention for the future. They are not statements that report observations of what is going on now, or predictions of what will happen based on evidence. Although they are truth-evaluable, and may be falsified if what is said is not what is the case, they are peculiar because they are the kinds of statements where, as Anscombe puts it, 'Theophrastus' principle' applies: if what is said is not what is the case, then the mistake is *in the performance*. In addition, both their justification and their contradiction are also special. The first is by reference to *reasons* for acting (as opposed to evidence or other reasons for believing that things are so). And the second requires a contradictory *intention*, rather than a report that things are not as the expression of intention says they are. That is what Anscombe means when she says that the contradiction of 'I am going to bed at midnight' is not 'You won't, for you never keep such resolutions' (inductive evidence) but rather 'You won't, for I am going to stop you' (contrary intention).[34]

Thus, the reasoning in practical reasoning is the same as in theoretical reasoning and what makes it *practical* is, first, that the point of the relevant reasoning is given by the goal that the reasoner seeks to realize by means of that reasoning and the subsequent action; second, that the premises of such reasoning show the goodness of the action to be undertaken; third, that the conclusions of such reasoning may be actions or decisions, which can be accompanied by expressions of intention, either *in* action, or for the future; and that these are justified, and might be

---

[34] See *Intention*, pp. 2–7 and 55.

contradicted, in ways that are not only peculiar to them (i.e. in ways that diverge from those found in theoretical reasoning), but are distinctively practical, in that they involve reference to reasons for *acting* and to expressions of *intention*, respectively.

2

AMBIVALENCE AND AUTHENTIC AGENCY

Laura W. Ekstrom

Abstract
It is common to believe that some of our concerns are deeper
concerns of ours than are others and that some of our attitudes are
central rather than peripheral to our psychological identity. What
is the best approach to characterizing depth or centrality to the
self? This chapter addresses the matter of the depth and authenticity of attitudes and the relation of this matter to the autonomy of
action. It defends a conception of the real self in terms of preferences and convictions that cohere in a particular structural sense.
It thereby gives content to the notion of wholeheartedness to which
various action theorists make appeal. The approach is defended in
part by an examination of how it handles the phenomenon of
ambivalence.[1]

Some people have a clear idea of who they are and what they want.
They experience little inner tension, and they resolutely pursue
their ambitions with largely unqualified devotion. Others are not
this way. We feel pulled in different directions. We have difficulty
figuring out how much we want to invest in various relationships,
and we experience confusion over which concerns and projects fit
most authentically in our lives. Augustine, in at least one period of
his life, seems to have fit in the latter category. In a famous passage
of his *Confessions,* he describes an experience of inner turmoil,
torn between his competing worldly temptations, on the one
hand, and his spiritual ambitions, including 'renunciation of this
world's joys,' on the other. He writes, 'My inner self was a house
divided against itself.' In the 'agony of indecision,' Augustine says,
'I tore my hair and hammered my forehead with my fists; I locked
my fingers and hugged my knees.' Though our own psychic con-

[1]   I have benefited from exchanges with Nomy Arpaly, Anthony Ellis, Keith Lehrer, Al
Mele, Eugene Mills, Eleonore Stump, and James S. Taylor. Earlier versions of this chapter
were presented at Florida State University and Virginia Commonwealth University. I am
grateful to audience members for their remarks. For helpful written comments on an early
version, I am particularly indebted to Brie Gertler and Justin Weinberg.

flicts may involve different types of concerns than these, the predicament of volitional paralysis Augustine describes is nonetheless familiar. Many of us understand what it is to be in a state of psychic discord, unable to move forward in any wholehearted way. Augustine calls the affliction 'a disease of the mind.'[2] We may call it simply ambivalence.

As a more ordinary illustration of the problem, consider an economist who desires, on the one hand, to speak her mind to a supercilious colleague. She wants to speak up because there would be satisfaction in pointing out to him her awareness of the fact that his behaviour, though superficially pleasant, is manipulative and condescending toward her. Yet at the same time, she is also inclined toward keeping her mouth shut, as doing so would promote the goal of keeping the departmental peace. She has been agreeable for years, and her being confrontational now would upset the *status quo*. Suppose that she is worked up in knots about the situation, so that interactions with this particular colleague are fraught with tension. 'Shall I unleash my thoughts or shall I remain outwardly pleasant?' she wonders. The problem is that she is not sure which of the contemplated courses of action she can throw herself behind and be wholehearted in pursuing. Suppose she seeks advice from a friend. He advises, 'go with your gut on this.' But that is precisely the problem, she thinks: what does my gut tell me? Or to switch metaphors, where does my heart lie? Or to drop the metaphors altogether, with respect to the desire to speak my mind and the desire to refrain, which is more authentic or true to myself?

Harry Frankfurt, in a series of influential papers spanning the past several decades, has drawn our attention to such cases, viewing them as an important subject of philosophical examination in the service of a full understanding of personal agency. Frankfurt has suggested that some of our attitudes and actions are more *our own* than are others, and his work on this matter has sparked debate on a cluster of related issues concerning *ownership* of desire, *identification* with certain attitudes, *alienation* from other attitudes, *authenticity, autonomy* of action, *wholeheartedness* in willing, and the condition of *ambivalence*. Augustine and the conflicted economist exhibit the latter, the condition of

---

[2]   *Confessions*, Book VIII, sections 8, 9 (New York: Penguin, 1961), pp. 170–72.

ambivalence. Sometimes, of course, we call people ambivalent toward a matter merely when they find it inconsequential and lack interest in any of the options (as a person might be ambivalent concerning multiple unattractive suitors). Ambivalence of the disinterested sort is not my focus here. It seems not particularly harmful to a person, although if sufficiently recurrent, it may undercut the engagement of the self with living that is part of human flourishing. The ambivalent person who does not care about much at all, we say, 'floats through life.' He is bland, uninteresting; he lacks a clear identity. Unless we ourselves are controlling, people like this make poor friends.

Ambivalence as understood here is, instead, a matter of having what some might call 'mixed feelings.' It includes the state of having unresolved attitudes both for and against a thing, as when one has both love and hate for a single person, or when one is both drawn to and repulsed by the same potential course of action. It also includes the state of having unresolved conflict between desires for incompatible things, where this conflict is unresolved because the ambivalent person has not determined what it is she truly wants. The person who is ambivalent in this sense experiences the stress of internal disunity.

What is the remedy for this situation? Augustine believed that one mired in internal conflict can only pray, for the sole antidote to ambivalence is a miracle. Is there any other means by which a person might take matters into her own hands and move beyond self-defeat? A closer look at the nature of internal conflict might guide us toward an answer. The structure of the remainder of the chapter is as follows. In section I, I focus on the notions of internal conflict and identification. In section II, I discuss reasons for rejecting a certain kind of approach to characterizing the real self. In section III, I develop an alternative conception of the self and suggest an account of self-directed action based upon it. Section IV develops a coherentist account of autonomous action with both procedural and structural elements. In sections V and VI, I work to recommend the account by showing that it both provides a deeper understanding of the phenomenon of ambivalence and points toward a way of overcoming it. The account of self-directed action developed here is thus not only of theoretical interest. It is also of practical interest: it shows how we can cope with what Augustine calls a disease of the mind.

I. Inner conflict and identification

To understand ambivalence as a matter of *inner conflict* requires some account of internality to an agent. Which attitudes count as internal? One simple answer is that *all* of an agent's psychological states are internal. The ambivalent person, on this proposal, is to be characterized as someone whose attitudes are mixed, where the content of 'whose attitudes' is fixed by the confines of some skull.

This simple proposal, however, has two problems. First, many contemporary philosophers construe mental states as relations to environmental facts outside the head. Second, the simple account does not capture the relevant intuitions. How so? The threat of misery inherent in ambivalence simply does not come from all of the attitudes that are internal in the 'boundaries of the head' sense. Fleeting desires – for instance, the desire to whack back after being whacked in the face, innocently perhaps, by a child playing – and beliefs that one adopts only for the sake of the argument – 'suppose that Schopenhauer's views concerning the capacities of women were true' – do not tie one up in knots, psychologically speaking. Since such attitudes are only 'loosely' possessed or, one might say, not really possessed at all, they cannot play a part in constituting *internal* conflicts. The loving parent experiences no ambivalence whatsoever in the face of an instinctual impulse to strike back after being hit in the face, accidentally or not, by her child, as the impulse is not in any significant way a part of who she is.

Furthermore, attitudes need not be fleeting in order to be external in the sense relevant to our discussion. Cases of particular interest in recent work in action theory involve persons who are alienated from attitudes that are 'theirs' only in the sense of being part of their, and not someone else's, mental life. There is a difference, important to our understanding of agency, between, on the one hand, the colleague considering his desire to enjoy another glass of wine with friends as against his desire for a non-alcoholic beverage, instead, given his plans to drive his friends home and, on the other, the man who feels the pull toward a glass of wine but who is self-distanced from the desire as part of his commitment to recover from alcoholism. Both experience the temptation of the wine, but in the first case it represents a live option about which the colleague might have some ambivalence, whereas in the second case it is a force the man views as

alien, such that he himself is entirely on the other side. Specification of the alienation at issue – or its converse, identification with
(or ownership of) desire – is difficult and contested.[3] It is nonetheless clear that, in the intuitive sense of 'internal conflict' at
work above, this term does not mean 'a conflict that occurs within
the agent's head.'[4]

I believe that if we had a plausible account of the nature of the
self, then we could bring the relevant internal/external distinction into clearer focus. We might use the account of the self to
make sense of cases in which the agent frustrates, rather than
expresses, her self in action, including cases in which coercion has
played no role in producing what the agent does. Furthermore,
since autonomy is self-government or *self-direction* – as opposed to
enslavement or rule-from-without – the account of what is internal
and what is external to the self should serve the project of constructing a good account of autonomous action.

To be clear: a defensible account of the self in the sense at issue
need not imply anything in particular for our ontology. It need
not, for instance, commit us to the existence of a trans-empirical
Self or a soul or a Cartesian mind or a special agential power to
cause events in a way that is not reducible to purely event-causal

---

[3]   For discussion, see Nomy Arpaly and Timothy Schroeder, 'Praise, Blame, and the
Whole Self,' *Philosophical Studies* 93 (1999): pp. 161–88; Michael Bratman, 'A Desire of
One's Own,' *Journal of Philosophy* 100, no. 5 (2003): pp. 221–42; Bratman, 'Identification,
Decision, and Treating as a Reason,' *Philosophical Topics*, vol. 24, no. 2 (1996): pp. 1–18;
Gerald Dworkin, *The Theory and Practice of Autonomy* (Cambridge: Cambridge University
Press, 1988); Laura Ekstrom, 'Alienation, Autonomy, and the Self,' *Midwest Studies in
Philosophy*, vol. 29 (2005): pp. 45–67; Ekstrom, 'Autonomy and Personal Integration,' in
James S. Taylor, ed., *Personal Autonomy* (Cambridge: Cambridge University Press, 2005), pp.
143–161; Ekstrom, 'A Coherence Theory of Autonomy,' *Philosophy and Phenomenological
Research* 53 (1993): pp. 599–616; Harry Frankfurt, 'Freedom of the Will and the Concept of
a Person,' *Journal of Philosophy* 68 (1971): pp. 5–20; Frankfurt, 'Identification and Exter-
nality,' in Frankfurt, *The Importance of What We Care About* (New York: Cambridge University
Press, 1988); Alfred Mele, *Autonomous Agents* (New York: Oxford University Press, 1995);
Richard Moran, 'Frankfurt on Identification: Ambiguities of Activity in Mental Life,' in
Sarah Buss and Lee Overton, eds., *Contours of Agency: Essays on Themes from Harry Frankfurt*
(Cambridge, MA: MIT Press, 2002), pp. 188–217; T. M. Scanlon, 'Reasons and Passions,' in
Buss and Overton, eds., (2002), pp. 165–183; J. David Velleman, 'Identification and
Identity,' in Buss and Overton, eds., (2002), pp. 91–123; Gary Watson, 'Free Agency,'
Journal of Philosophy 72 (1975): pp. 205–220.

[4]   Many of us rely roughly on an inside/outside the head distinction in understanding
the term 'coercion' as applying to various methods of 'external' interference with agency,
including the various forms of manipulation by 'outside' persons and forces: brainwashing,
indoctrination, threats, and posthypnotic suggestion. However, there is reason to acknowledge another sense in which forces inside the head can, like coercive forces, interfere with
agency.

terms. The self at issue is, rather, a kind of psychological essence.[5] We gesture at our commitment to such essences when we describe cases of personal transformation, as in, 'he is no longer himself, since inheriting a lot of money' and 'she is not the person she used to be since her life-changing cancer treatment.' In speaking this way, we are not making unusual metaphysical claims, but rather we are remarking on significant changes in moral or psychological identity.[6] Augustine's struggle, for instance, is clearly not one of sorting out his metaphysical identity – he might be a living physical organism, no matter what he wills or thinks – but it is, instead, one of identifying his true will, or determining what is central to himself in a psychological sense.

Notice that it often seems appropriate to say that some elements of a person's psychology are more central, while others are peripheral. The concern a parent has to promote the health and well-being of his children, we say, is a deep concern of his, one central to his identity. The value a philosopher places on her research program might be central to who she is, whereas the belief that it would be good to get some physical exercise might in her case be peripheral. Settling on the right way to account for this difference in depth or centrality would be useful both to broader projects of understanding human agency and autonomy and, more particularly, to understanding the phenomenon of ambivalence.

II. Features of a successful account

One familiar approach to dealing with the conflict among desires inherent in ambivalence begins by emphasizing our ability to mentally 'rise above' our desires and to reflect upon them, asking ourselves not only what we want to do, but also what we want to desire and upon which desires we want to act. These latter desires – labeled 'second-order,' in virtue of their having as intentional objects *other* desires (or states of affairs involving those desires) – rather than the 'first-order' ones – that is, desires to perform or

[5]   See Susan Wolf's discussion of the real self in her *Freedom Within Reason* (New York: Oxford University Press, 1990) and Robert Kane's notion of a 'self-network' in his *The Significance of Free Will* (New York: Oxford University Press, 1996).
[6]   For discussion, see Velleman, 'Identification and Identity,' in Buss and Overton, eds., 2002, pp. 91–123; and Frankfurt, 'Reply to J. David Velleman,' 2002, pp. 124–128.

not to perform certain acts – are taken by some theorists to constitute the agent's authentic perspective.

One perceived benefit of this widely-admired hierarchical approach to identifying what an agent *truly wants* is that it seems to distinguish reasons for acting that have their source in the agent's activity from mere impulses.[7] First-level desires appear, on Frankfurt's prominent view, to be mere pulls or temptations toward performing some action or other, and while such impulses might on occasion be voluntarily adopted, normally they simply arise unbidden. Further, such desires may or may not be attitudes the agent takes to count as reasons for acting or for deliberating in particular ways.[8] By contrast, higher-order attitudes may seem in their very formation to involve the agent's activity. For instance, if it is a cold day, one might find oneself wanting to drink some hot tea, in a natural drive to maintain stable body temperature, although, ordinarily, one does not 'find oneself' *wanting to want* to drink hot tea or wanting the desire to drink hot tea to play a role in motivationally-effective practical reasoning. It would apparently take some activity on one's part to generate such a second-order mental state, and so the second-order desire might seem to reflect, more deeply than does the first-order one, who one is.

Despite this and other attractions of the approach appealing to higher-order desires, it is not clear that there are satisfactory responses to a variety of problems for it, including prominently a regress of desires conferring the status of internality on the desires which are their objects.[9] Notice that the regress is not only a problem because one might happen to experience conflict at a

[7]   Although many (including Scanlon 2002 and Moran 2002) have read Frankfurt as suggesting that second-order states have authenticity in virtue of their being actively generated by the agent, Frankfurt has made clear that, in his view, higher-order attitudes are not essentially active. One may passively identify with a lower-level state, Frankfurt believes, for instance, in exhaustion. See Buss and Overton, eds., 2002, p. 90, note 2 and p. 225, note 1.

[8]   Concerning first-order desires, the way Frankfurt now expresses the point is that a desire presents an agent not with a reason but with a problem, the problem of what to do with it: identify with it, throwing one's weight behind it, so to speak, or reject it as an outlaw. He distinguishes four steps in the process of responding to this problem. See his 'Reply to Michael E. Bratman' in Buss and Overton, eds., 2002, pp. 86–9.

[9]   For discussion, see Bratman, 'A Desire of One's Own;' Ekstrom, 'A Coherence Theory of Autonomy' and 'Alienation, Autonomy, and the Self;' Adrian Piper, 'Two Conceptions of the Self,' *Philosophical Studies* 48 (1985): pp. 173–197; Eleonore Stump, 'Sanctification, Hardening of the Heart, and Frankfurt's Concept of Free Will,' *Journal of Philosophy* 85 (1988): pp. 395–412; Watson, 'Free Agency,' and 'Free Action and Free Will,' *Mind* XCVI (1987): pp. 145–72.

variety of levels and so be driven to form desires about desires about desires, and so on. Rather, the regress is a theoretical one generated by the characterization of internality itself. Attempts to cut off the regress at one level or another are subject to charges of arbitrariness, as is Frankfurt's characterization of internality to the self in terms of *satisfaction*, construed as a state of the entire psychic system, 'a state constituted just by the absence of any tendency or inclination to alter its condition.'[10] In more recent work, Frankfurt sets out an account of identification as *acceptance*, rather than as the type of positive endorsement that generates a regress.[11] This move makes clear that Frankfurt does not, in fact, require *reflective endorsement* of a desire for identification of the real self with it.

The move to acceptance, as opposed to normative evaluation or endorsement, does not do the trick, however. Some explanations for the required acceptance – including exhaustion, external manipulation, boredom and frustration, all permitted by Frankfurt – are intuitively not the kind of states and processes that can confer the status of authenticity or internality on an agent's desires. Why should we think that a certain act – flopping on the sofa while my toddler takes a bath without my supervision, for instance – is what I 'really want' if I accept the desire for doing so only because I am too exhausted or too distracted to think any harder about the matter? Even worse, why think so if my acceptance traces to the hypnotic influence of someone who wishes my child harm? After sufficient rest, I might be startled by the attitudes I was earlier willing to accept. Certain reasons for joining oneself to a desire – not only external manipulation, but also guilt, laziness and inattention – are intuitively autonomy-undermining. This casts doubt on Frankfurt's claim that the source of an agent's acceptance of her desires is irrelevant.[12]

What I believe we have learned from the literature on the hierarchical approach is that a good account of authentic agency will have the following features. It will (i) clearly identify the elements that constitute the real self, (ii) explain which features

[10]   Frankfurt, 'The Faintest Passion,' 1999, p. 104.
[11]   See Buss and Overton, eds., *Contours of Agency*, 2002, especially pp. 160–1.
[12]   See Frankfurt, 'Reply to John Martin Fischer,' in Buss and Overton, eds., 2002, p. 27. For critical discussion see, for instance, Watson, 'Free Action and Free Will;' Dworkin, *The Theory and Practice of Autonomy;* and Gideon Yaffe, 'Free Agency at Its Best,' *Philosophical Perspectives* 14, *Action and Freedom*, 2000, pp. 210–213.

of those elements ground or make non-arbitrary their claim to
authenticity, (iii) avoid a problematic regress in accounting for
authenticity, and (iv) rule out coerced (or externally manipu-
lated) attitudes as sources of truly self-direction action.

III. The nature of the self

In 'Free Agency,' Gary Watson proposed that we act in a way that
is self-directed when we act on values, which derive from Reason
rather then Appetite. Crucial to our free agency, Watson urged
(*contra* Frankfurt in his 'Freedom of the Will and the Concept of
a Person') is not that we be moved to act by a desire for which we
have a higher-order desire, but rather that we be moved by
general principles we could defend in a cool and non-self-
deceptive moment. Despite Watson's own later repudiation of this
view as excessively rationalistic, I believe that progress can indeed
be made toward clarifying *agential internality* in part by focusing
on desires that are grounded in reflection on what is good or of
value. Suppose we apply the label 'preferences' to desires that
have been formed by way of, or have withstood, a process of
critical evaluation with regard to the agent's conception of the
good.[13] If an agent deliberates about what to do or what to desire,
considers various relevant factors including her convictions concerning what is good, and as the outcome of that consideration
reflectively endorses a certain desire or course of action, then the
outcome of the decision – its settlement state – is a preference in
our sense. In relying on the stipulative definition of preference,
the idea is to demarcate the boundaries of an agent's psychological identity in part by a certain type of attitude, leaving other sorts
outside. The former are the considered or reflectively evaluated
desires ('preferences'), and the latter are the inclinations,
instincts, urges and fancies that impel by sheer force, apart from
the operation of evaluative reflection.

In constructing a picture of the self, why should we favor a
Watsonian emphasis on *evaluative endorsement*, rather than a Frank-

---

[13] The notion that one has a conception of the good need only imply that one has
cognitive attitudes of assent to propositions concerning the nature and quality of various
experiences, courses of action, and other ends. The phrase should be taken neither to rule
out that one's conception might be multi-faceted and variable through time, nor to suggest
that it involve either a prescription that others adopt its components or an expectation that
all other rational agents would agree.

furtian emphasis on *acceptance* of one's desires for any reason whatsoever? I believe that the reflective process involved in the formation of preference is crucial because our critical engagement with the question of what we have good reason to do, our evaluation of desires and courses of action with respect to worth, and our endorsement of some of these – these activities are widely and rightly viewed as constituting the participation of the self. Such a view is indeed rationalistic, if by that we mean that it takes as essential to our authentic agency the exercise of our ability for evaluative reasoning and critical assessment. Notice, though, that nothing in the understanding of preferences as reflectively evaluated desires requires them to be higher-order attitudes.[14] A preference, as we use the term here, is identified as such not by its type of intentional object, but rather by the process through which it was generated or is maintained.

Preferences are surely not the sole elements of the self. I have made appeal, in describing their formation, to one's convictions concerning what is good or of value. If we call 'beliefs' the wide class of states of mental assent to propositions (including assent to some propositions out of guilt or simply for argument's sake or out of threat for non-compliance), then we may use the term 'conviction' to mark the mental endorsement of a proposition formed by critical reflection with the aim of assenting to what is true.[15] Since it represents an agent's attempt at accurately understanding the world, a conviction has a better claim to representing who a person really is, than does a mere belief. Convictions certainly should play a role in the appropriate conception of the self, augmenting attitudes of preference. Such attitudes feature in the characterization of who one is – they help to pick out the individual who is oneself. We use the notion of the self, after all, to refer to the complex of attributes or features that mark and distinguish an individual from others.

It is appropriate and useful on my view, then, to consider the self in a psychological sense to be an aggregate of attitudes of

[14]   In 'A Desire of One's Own,' Bratman argues that higher-order Frankfurtian commitments might be involved, in certain cases, in giving an account of why different decisions are made by persons in similar circumstances who share the same value judgments. The argument in my view, however, does not show that such higher-order states must be involved in a defensible account of the difference between the two cases.

[15]   Lehrer calls these latter states 'acceptances.' Given Frankfurt's use of the term 'acceptance' to mark an entirely different phenomenon, I use here the term 'conviction' to refer to the relevant beliefs. See Lehrer's *Theory of Knowledge* (Boulder, CO: Westview, 1990).

preference and conviction, together with a faculty for fashioning and refashioning those attitudes by evaluation with respect to truth and value. It is a short step from this proposed conception of the self to a basic theory of autonomy. Since autonomy is self-direction, relying on the proposed description of the self yields the following result: An act is self-directed just in case it springs (non-deviantly) from a preference, and in forming and in acting upon this preference one was not the victim of coercion.[16] Call this the *basic autonomy theory*. Since the capacity for critical reflection is partially constitutive of one's moral or psychological identity, one's exercises of this capacity are one's own, barring external manipulation by way of coercive mechanisms. One might propose that the marriage between Appetite and Reason captured by the basic theory is sufficient for autonomous action. The basic autonomy theory is indeed a plausible view that may be sufficient for some contexts. I want to suggest, further, that we add a structural coherence requirement to yield a richer account of autonomous action. In the following section, I describe this richer account. In the subsequent two sections, I discuss the matter of its application.

IV. The coherence theory of autonomous action

I understand the coherence among preferences and convictions relevant to the coherence theory of autonomy I want to defend not in a minimal sense of lack of conflict, but rather in a fuller sense of defensibility and mutual support.[17] Let us say that a preference P is *personally authorized* for a person at a time (or counts as 'truly her own' or is representative of her real self) to the extent that the preference coheres with her system of other preferences and convictions at that time. A preference P *coheres* with the system of convictions and preferences of a person at a time to

---

[16] I take it that one is not a 'victim of coercion' if the coercive mechanism is something for which one has previously autonomously arranged. See Mele, *Autonomous Agents*.

[17] Lehrer's theory of epistemic justification provides a useful model of this coherence, as it envisions justification centrally as a contest with a skeptical interlocutor who challenges one's beliefs. On the account, roughly, a state of acceptance is justified just in case it coheres with whatever else the believer accepts, and an acceptance coheres just in case it can be defended against skeptical challenges by the believer's other acceptances. See Lehrer (1990).

the extent that, for a competing preference, it is either more valuable for the person to have P than to have the competing preference on the basis of her system at the time, or it is as valuable for her to have the competing preference and a neutralizing attitude, as it is for her to have the competing preference alone, on the basis of the system at the time.[18] One preference *competes* with another preference for a person at a time just in case it is less valuable for that person to have the preference on the assumption that the object of the other is good than on the assumption that the object of the other is bad, relative to her system of preferences and convictions at a time.

The following is an example of how one can meet the challenge of a competing preference by defeating it. Suppose I have a desire to enjoy a week of vacation in the Cayman Islands. Suppose I also have a desire to spend that same week of vacation in New York City. I only have one week of vacation. I must select a location. The desire to vacation in New York might survive a process of reflective evaluation with respect to the good, so that it qualifies as a preference. Suppose that it does, and that the desire to vacation in the Cayman Islands also survives a process of reflective evaluation with respect to the good, so that it, too, qualifies as a preference. In acting on which preference would I be most true to myself? Suppose that, for me, the preference to vacation in the Cayman Islands is defensible by a network of supporting convictions and preferences. This is the case because, suppose, I am convinced that I am in need of relaxation and that I experience more relaxation in a warm climate than a cold one. While I know that in New York I could see friends and find more intellectual stimulation, I am nonetheless convinced that, at the moment, I am rather over-stimulated, tired, and in need of some peace and quiet. Further, I love to snorkel, and a favorite activity of mine is reading on a sandy beach, looking out at the smooth aqua expanse of the Caribbean Sea. I am convinced that I would not be able to enjoy those activities in New York, and so on. Thus while I do have a preference to visit New York, nonetheless, that preference does not cohere as well as its competitor does with the elements of my self at the particular

---

[18] For elaboration and different articulations, see Ekstrom 'A Coherence Theory of Autonomy' and 'Alienation, Autonomy, and the Self,' in which it is explained how a neutralizing attitude can work to make a preference that is initially competing no longer a competitor.

time in question, given the overall considerations. The competing preference – to spend the week in New York, instead – is defeated.

On the coherence theory of autonomy I recommend, then, an autonomous act is one non-deviantly caused by a preference (i) that has been formed or is maintained without the coercive influence of another agent (for which the agent herself has not autonomously arranged), and (ii) that coheres with his other preferences and convictions. The suggestion is that, while the self includes all of one's preferences and convictions, only some of these are aspects of what we might call one's real or authentic self. The coherence autonomy account depicts autonomous acts as deriving from only certain psychological attitudes, those of the real self.

Why should we adopt a structural coherence account of the elements of the real self? One consideration is that we tend to view the more enduring aspects of a person's psychology as central, rather than peripheral, to who he is. Since, as I conceive of the relevant coherence, cohering elements of one's psychology display consistency and mutual support, they tend to be particularly long-lasting. Preferences and convictions bound together in joint reinforcement tend not to be in perpetual flux. Unfortunately, however, sometimes non-cohering, repudiated aspects of oneself (such as the desire to binge in the bulimic who hates his condition) are painfully long-lasting. Persistence through time, then, cannot be the sole consideration in establishing depth of an attitude to the psychological self.

A second consideration is that we tend to think of a person's real or authentic self as the collection of attributes that make sense in light of each other and that can be appealed to in the project of mutual defense against neurotic doubt and against challenge by other individuals. The cohering elements of one's psychology are fully defensible by reference to other elements. That is, in the face of challenges by other people – such as 'that's not really what you think, is it?' or 'why do you want that?' – the cohering elements of one's psychology may come into play, so that the attitudes in question may come to be seen by others as making sense, given one's other preferences and convictions. The cohering elements are not odd or anomalous attitudes that the agent cannot explain or defend. Rather, they fit with, in fact they constitute, her 'party line.'

Finally, we tend to think of someone's real self as comprised of attitudes with which he is for the most part comfortable and to which he is especially attached, though problem cases involving embarrassment, denial and self-deception challenge this consideration. I think we should spell out the relevant attachment not in an affective way (his authentic attitude is not the one he *feels most strongly* about), but rather in terms of structural integration with other relevant attitudes, on the metaphor of a tightly interwoven tapestry. One tends not to have distress over attitudes that cohere with one's other considered attitudes, as one might have distress or consternation over incoherent or anomalous attitudes. Since the coherent elements fit with the other preferences and convictions, in acting on them, one is not frustrated or in tumult but rather enjoys a kind of liberating comfort with oneself.

I have suggested that Frankfurt's response to the regress problem for hierarchical accounts is unsuccessful, since certain explanations of one's alleged regress-ending acceptance of one's desires fail to ground their authenticity. Our alternative response to the regress problem for the authenticity of desire draws on a strategy for avoiding a regress of reasons familiar from the epistemological literature: we view the structure of reasons as a web, an interweaving structure of mutual support.[19] Our understanding of coherence is a matter of mental states' fitting together, clinging to or supporting each other, thereby giving particular content to an appeal, made similarly by some other autonomy theorists, to an ideal of agential wholeheartedness or personal integration.[20] One might give an affective or feeling-based account of wholeheartedness. My approach has been, rather, to provide a structural account with procedural elements.

V. Complexity and worth

Some may find the suggested account of autonomous action too complex. Nomy Arpaly, for instance, has written that, since the coherence autonomy theory proposes fairly strict conditions, 'autonomy, as Ekstrom defines it, is a bit like happiness or fitness: an eminently reasonable thing to which to aspire, but not the

[19] For reasons to reject a foundationalist approach, see Ekstrom 'Keystone Preferences and Autonomy,' *Philosophy and Phenomenological Research*, LIX (1999): pp. 1057–1063.

[20] See Harry Frankfurt, 'Identification and Wholeheartedness,' and Nomy Arpaly and Timothy Schroeder, 'Praise, Blame, and the Whole Self.'

34 LAURA W. EKSTROM

default condition of human beings.'[21] However, Arpaly continues, if the account does not depict a default condition of human beings, then how can it be of use, for instance, in medical contexts, in which patient autonomy is supposed to ground certain practitioner obligations? Furthermore, interest in autonomy has been driven in large measure by interest in moral responsibility, yet it is unclear how, given its complexity, the coherence account of autonomy might relate to such issues. For instance, *Crime and Punishment*'s torn Raskolnivkov may not, on the account, be a legitimate candidate for blame for the murder he commits. This may seem counterintuitive. As Arpaly rightly points out, nonetheless, 'this is not a problem for Ekstrom's view, because she does not argue that we are only responsible for actions that meet her conditions.'[22]

The challenge, then, is to explain what intuitions the coherence account of autonomy is designed to capture, since it does not depict a default feature of all human beings in virtue of which their rights deserve respect, and it is not designed fundamentally to capture intuitions about morally responsible agency. Of course, a complex autonomy theory, as Arplay admits, 'can be valuable and interesting even if it has nothing to do with moral responsibility or, for that matter, with applied ethics, for of course there is more to the philosophical study of the vagaries of the human heart than what is contained in these subjects.'[23] Nonetheless, the challenge remains to ground the account and to demonstrate its worth.

My response is as follows. First, the dismissal of the coherence theory as irrelevant to moral responsibility may be too swift. On one approach to moral responsibility, the praiseworthiness or blameworthiness of an agent for performing a certain action is measured by several factors: one, the moral desirability of the action itself, whether it is right or wrong and to what extent; two, the agent's reasons for performing the act; and three, how 'deep' those reasons are to the agent's psychology.[24] Someone who acts charitably from a motivation that is shallow to her self is less

---

[21] Arpaly, 'Responsibility, Applied Ethics, and Complex Autonomy Theories,' in *Personal Autonomy*, ed. James S. Taylor (New York: Cambridge University Press, 2005), p. 164.
[22] Ibid., p. 195.
[23] Ibid., p. 165.
[24] See Arpaly, 'Moral Worth,' *Journal of Philosophy* 99 (2002): pp. 223–245; and Arpaly, *Unprincipled Virtue* (New York: Oxford University Press, 2002).

praiseworthy, on this sort of view, than is someone whose motivation toward charity is a deeper element of her self. The amount of praise or blame people deserve varies with the depth of their motivations or the extent of their indifference.[25]

Arpaly herself defends such an approach to moral responsibility. Thus, she is committed to two important claims, as are proponents of the sort of view she sets out. First, the approach relies on the contention that some desires (concerns) are deeper or more central to a person's moral or psychological identity than are others. Second, Arpaly and those like-minded concerning moral responsibility are committed to the claim that the depth of a desire (concern) is a matter of degree. The theory of moral worth is thus *in need of an account of the deep or real self*, as it views persons as candidates for legitimate praise or blame when their actions derive from that self. I have provided here one such account. Given the close connection Arpaly and other moral responsibility theorists draw between moral responsibility and self-expression, the coherence account of the central self might prove useful.

Setting aside the potential relevance to issues of moral responsibility, my second response to the challenge of grounding the coherence theory of autonomy is this. Acting autonomously is an antidote to passivity and victimization – it is a way of asserting our selves into the world. One source of interest in autonomy is a desire to make our lives more our own and less at the mercy of fortune, fate, and the control of others. What grounds the coherence theory of autonomy, then, is the set of intuitions we have used in settling on plausible accounts of the self and of depth of an attitude to the self. Furthermore, the *usefulness* of the account is its depiction for us of an agential ideal. Were we to get ourselves to form and to act upon personally authorized preferences – that is, cohering ones – we would thereby obtain some peace of mind. The account depicts an aspect of the good life, something to which we can aspire.

The account may, as well, provide a model for understanding an important aspect of self-love. On Aquinas's conception of love as developed by Eleonore Stump, love is understood to involve crucially the lover's desire for the good of the beloved and the

----

[25] Arpaly, *Unprincipled Virtue*, p. 115.

lover's desire for union with the beloved.[26] Given this approach to the nature of love, Stump suggests, self-love is, in part, a matter of being united to oneself or having internal integration. The accounts of the self and of the real self I have defended provide a model of such personal integration and wholeheartedness.

VI. Coping with ambivalence

Finally, the coherence theory of autonomy has worth in providing guidance for coping with the problem of ambivalence. Recall the case of the economist torn between her desire to confront her manipulative colleague and her opposing desire to remain silent. How should this individual remain true to herself as she decides what to do?

Suppose that both the desire to speak up and the desire to keep her mouth shut survive an evaluative reflective process that takes into account her convictions concerning what is good. She sees value in both desires and in both of the courses of action they recommend. She is convinced that it is good to be assertive and to stand up for oneself and, at the same time, she knows the worth of appropriate self-censure and tact. Both desires, then, count as preferences and hence as parts of herself – this is precisely the nature of her internal conflict. Her will is divided.

Suppose that for this particular individual, however, the preference for keeping her mouth shut in the circumstances coheres best overall with her system of convictions and preferences, in that they support its value over that of the competing preference. To fill in how this works, suppose that she is convinced that the manipulative colleague in question is a defensive, unreasonable person prone to both outbursts of anger and long bouts of resentment. Suppose further that she accepts that the personality traits of some individuals do not enable them to deal productively with conflict and to treat others with appropriate respect. Furthermore, she is convinced that she herself is not likely to be able to forget the unpleasant conversation, were it to occur, since she will repeatedly mentally replay what was said. Suppose she prefers to save her battles for those with whom she sees more potential for meaningful relationships. She also prefers to work in an environment characterized by at least superficial peace and not in one filled with overt rudeness and anger. She is convinced as well that, if she were to speak her mind, the consequent responses would be harmful to her department colleagues and to her institution.

Relative to this individual's system of preferences and convictions, then – no matter how someone else might decide the matter – the preference for remaining silent concerning the behaviour of her colleague coheres. It counts as an attitude that is authentic and central to her identity. Thus, assuming the preference has not been coercively imposed, for her it is a source of autonomous action. When she deliberately keeps her mouth shut rather than taking the opportunities that arise to speak up on this particular matter, she acts in a way that is truly self-directed.

We desired at the outset to find a way out of the condition of ambivalence. We have found a way that is, I believe, superior to the direction other approaches would give. An overly simple view of our psychology understands disunity in the self as a matter of conflict between desires to act in various ways, and it offers as a way out of the conflict a sheer exertion of will in one direction or another. We want to be careful, though, to avoid two silly ideas: one, that there is a little agent in the head (or an 'eye' in the I) choosing one desire over another; and two, the idea that desire conflict resolution is accomplished by *sheer fiat* in a way that gives us no confidence that our ambivalence has been authentically resolved, or, to put it another way, that we have settled on what it is we really want. A somewhat more expansive simple view would see all of an agent's psychological states as internal to her, not only the desires to act. We have seen reason, though, to reject an account of internality that draws the boundaries of the self at the boundaries of the head.

Hierarchical accounts offered a potentially more satisfying picture: they allowed us to move from understanding disunity in the self as a matter of conflict between first-level desires to a conception appealing to a lack of mesh between second-level attitudes and first-level ones, suggesting the following solution to the problem of ambivalence. When torn among competing desires to do this and that, one might form higher-order volitions concerning the lower-level attitudes. The idea is that higher-order volitions allow us to settle on an identity, by 'putting our weight behind' certain attitudes and not others. Because the attitudes that we reject are no longer internal, they cannot fuel internal conflicts. We have, then, lessened our ambivalence. The adequacy of the hierarchical account of the way out of ambivalence depends on the plausibility of taking higher-order volitions to constitute the agent's authentic perspective and so to be the source of her autonomous action. Many have argued that this claim is suspect.

The accounts of the self and of the central self I have defended both provide a model of personal integration and explain the nature of internal conflict. Desires that are not preferences, and beliefs that are not convictions, are not internal to the self. But preferences and convictions are aspects of the self, and these might be in tension. In providing an account of the real or central self as one consisting of certain cohering mental states, and in giving substance to the relevant notion of coherence, I have pointed toward a means for making one's actions lead in a consistent direction, as an antidote to self-defeat.

VII. Conclusion

A person might save himself from the unhappiness of internal conflict by disengaging from cares, but only at the cost of a sort of aloofness or detachment that seems not emblematic of a full personal life. Any better direction we can find in avoiding the condition of ambivalence should contribute toward our building lives that are meaningful and, importantly, our own. The ambivalence of internal conflict is not, *contra* Augustine, surmountable only by way of a miracle. To deal with it, first, one can actively form preferences to move beyond mere desires. Second, one can attempt to form and to revise one's preference structure with an eye toward coherence, understood as defensibility in the face of challenge and mutual support. Third, one can act on cohering preferences. The escape from ambivalence requires both introspective reflective ability and willpower, understood as the exercise of the capacity of choice toward the ends one views as appropriate. We have, then, some hope for dealing with what Augustine called a disease of the mind.

3

THE ROAD TO LARISSA

John Hyman

Abstract
In the *Meno*, Socrates asks why knowledge is a better guide to acting the right way than true belief. The answer he proposes is ingenious, but it fails to solve the puzzle, and some recent attempts to solve it also fail. I shall argue that the puzzle cannot be solved as long as we conceive of knowledge as a kind of belief, or allow our conception of knowledge to be governed by the contrast between knowledge and belief.

§1 Traditionally, the story that opens chapter three of Genesis is called *The Fall*. But in his remarkable series of lectures, *Civil Disobedience in Antiquity*, David Daube argues that it should be called the story of the Rise. Adam and Eve, he says, are 'probably among the earliest heroes of civil disobedience', ethically as well as biologically the ancestors of Mahatma Gandhi and Martin Luther King. 'It is only if we read [Genesis 3] through late Jewish rabbinical and Christian spectacles that it is about a fall.'

In the Christian tradition, both the traditional name and the interpretation of the story associated with it were made canonical by Augustine's commentary in *The City of God*. Augustine's interpretation, although not the name of the story, derives essentially from Paul (*Romans*, 5.12-21). It is as follows.

Before they ate the knowledge-giving fruit, Adam and Eve were, we are told in the last verse of chapter two, "naked and not ashamed". (According to Augustine, their nakedness was not shameful because "not yet did lust move those members [i.e. the genitals] without the will's consent". (*City of God*, 14.17))

The devil, a fallen angel, envious of man's innocent and unfallen state, chose the serpent to 'insinuate his persuasive guile into the mind of man' because 'being slippery, and moving in tortuous windings, it was suitable for his purpose.' (14.11) The serpent, Augustine says, 'first tried his deceit upon the woman, making his assault upon the weaker part of that human alliance',

Agents and Their Actions, First Edition. Edited by Maximilian de Gaynesford. © 2011 Blackwell Publishing Ltd. Published 2011 by Blackwell Publishing Ltd.

(14.11) judging that the man might be more suceptible to persuasion by the woman than by himself. God had told Adam he would die if he ate the fruit, but Eve was persuaded by the serpent that the threat was empty, and that if she ate the fruit she would herself become like a god. Adam was not persuaded, but he yielded to Eve, 'the husband to the wife, the one human being to the only other human being.' (14.11)

Thus Eve was deceived, whereas Adam, Augustine says, 'sinned with his eyes open.' 'Although they were not both deceived by credulity, yet both were entangled in the snares of the devil and taken by sin.' (14.11)

What sin did Adam and Eve commit? It was the sin of pride. 'The evil act had never been done' Augustine says, 'had not an evil will preceded it. And what is the origin of our evil will but pride? And what is pride but the craving for undue exaltation.' (14.13) The immediate result of their sin was that their eyes were opened, they saw that they were naked, they were ashamed, and they covered the shameful parts of their bodies with fig-leaves.

Augustine acknowledges that it may not be immediately obvious to everyone who hears the story that Adam and Eve committed an act of 'great wickedness' (14.12). But he insists that we should not think that the sin was a small and light one, because it was committed about food. On the contrary, 'obedience is the mother and guardian of all the virtues', and preferring to fulfil one's own will, instead of the Creator's, 'is destruction.' (14.12)

Adam and Eve, Augustine says, 'despised the authority of God'; and God's punishment was that man would henceforth live 'in a hard and miserable bondage [since he had chosen obedience to his own will rather than to God's], doomed in spite of himself to die in body as he had willingly become dead in spirit, condemned even to eternal death (had not the grace of God delivered him) because he had forsaken eternal life.' (14.15) Augustine summarizes his interpretation of the story as follows:

> [Adam and Eve] committed so great a sin, that by it human nature was altered for the worse, and was transmitted also to their posterity, liable to sin and subject to death. (14.1)

This is the orthodox interpretation of the story in the Christian tradition, and the canonical interpretation in the Roman Catholic church. The interpretation in the Jewish tradition has been similar since the rabbinical period – in other words, for the last two thousand years.

§2 Here is what Daube says about the story of the Fall:

In the Greek myth, as Zeus, the highest of the gods, is intent on withholding from man the basic material for civilization, namely fire, Prometheus, a being half-way between the Olympian rulers and the earth-dwellers, steals the forbidden object from heaven and brings it to man. Zeus cannot undo what has been done; he can only inflict dire punishment on the two conspirators, Prometheus and man. The myth reflects an archaic phase in theology when man looks on the gods as opposed to him. Nor can one be surprised that there should have been such a phase seeing that, before the advent of even primitive technology, it must have been very natural for man to feel himself in the midst of a largely inimical set-up. Any gains were to be attained in defiance of the dominant forces around him.

In the Bible, one of the chapters representing this stage is the so-called story of the Fall. It is indeed astonishing that the true meaning should have been successfully supressed so long ... Stripped of subsequent interpretation, the narrative reports that Adam and Eve were in a garden, living crudely and mindlessly like the animals surrounding them. 'They were naked and not ashamed' – this, from the wisdom narrator's point of view, was not a blissful Rousseauesque state but a horrible primitivity. However, there was a tree in the garden with knowledge-giving fruit. Only God forbade the couple to eat of it, and he made sure his prohibition would be heeded by threatening them with immediate death if they disobeyed: 'On the day that you eat thereof, you shall assuredly die.' A being half-way between God and man, the serpent, informs them that this threat is empty: the fruit is not death-bringing, not fatal, on the contrary it will open their eyes and make them discerning. So they do eat of it, and indeed God turns out to have been lying. They do not die, and their eyes are opened exactly as the serpent, the Prometheus of the Biblical story, told them. They become discriminating between good and evil, aware of their nakedness – capable of shame. Just like Zeus, God inflicts fearful retribution on the rebellious serpent and couple, but like Zeus, he must put up with the start of human civilization.[1]

Perhaps Daube's suggestion that the story should be called *The Rise* is an exaggeration. It is true that the Hebrew word for fall (*nepilah*) does not occur in the story itself, or in any of the references to it in the Hebrew scriptures. And the story does not seem to describe a change for the worse in human nature. But it certainly does describe a change for the worse in the circumstances in which human beings live, and it explains the most difficult and painful aspects of human life, as well as the origin of civilization. Nevertheless, Daube's interpretation of the story is essentially correct.

First, as Daube says, nakedness was certainly considered shameful by the author of the story, and the community in which it was told and written down. It is extraordinary that commentators continue to miss this point. For example, the *New Cambridge Bible Commentary* on Genesis, published in 2008, tells us: 'Genesis 2 ends in a brief notation about the innocence of the first human couple. Although they were "naked" there was no shame in it.'[2] But this is not what the verse says. It does not say 'there was no shame in it'; it says, 'And they were both naked, the man and his wife, and not ashamed', which is of course quite different.

Second, there is no mention in the story of the devil. Satan appears in Jewish writings in the post-exilic period, about four centuries after Genesis was composed; and there, in the *Book of Job* for example, he is clearly subordinate to God and unable to act without his permission. Satan emerges as an independent personality, and as the personification of evil, in the first century AD, and the earliest extant statement in Jewish writings that he was responsible for the Fall is by Rabbi Eliezer, in the late first or early second century.

Third, Augustine seems to have believed that what mattered about the serpent is that he is slippery and moves in tortuous windings. In the text, by contrast, he is described as *arum*, which means, crafty, shrewd or cunning. *Arum* does not mean wicked or evil, any more than the Greek word *polymetis*, which Homer uses as

[1] David Daube, *Civil Disobedience in Antiquity* (Edinburgh: Edinburgh Univ. Press, 1972), pp. 60–61.
[2] Bill T. Arnold, *Genesis: New Cambridge Bible Commentary* (Cambridge: CUP, 2008), p. 61.

Odysseus's epithet. One thing that is made clear in the text is that the serpent knows that the humans will not die upon eating the forbidden fruit, but will become 'like Gods, knowing good and evil' (3.5), as God himself acknowledges they have done: 'Behold, the man is become as one of us, to know good and evil.' (3.22)

Fourth, the orthodox interpretation of the story disregards God's lie. God says to Adam: 'of the tree of the knowledge of good and evil, thou shalt not eat of it: for in the day that thou eatest thereof thou shalt surely die.' (2.17) The serpent says: 'Ye shall not surely die.' (3.4) And this is true. Ever since Paul, the orthodox interpretation has finessed this point by interpreting 'die' as 'become mortal' or 'become susceptible to eternal death'. But this is unconvincing. 'Die' is not used to mean these things elsewhere in the Hebrew scriptures. Besides, the creation story does not imply that Adam and Eve were immortal until God punished them for eating the fruit. On the contrary, God expels Adam from the Garden of Eden to ensure that he will not *become* immortal, by eating from the tree of life. (3.22-3)

Fifth, it cannot have been wicked or sinful on the part of Adam and Eve to eat the fruit of the tree of knowledge, because when they ate the fruit they did not yet know the difference between good and evil. It is true that they knew they were disobeying God. The story implies that this is something one can know without yet understanding evil, wickedness or sin. And no doubt this is correct. But disobedience in a state of moral innocence or ignorance, even deliberate disobedience – for example, by young children – is not evil, wicked or sinful, regardless of whom one disobeys.

Sixth, knowledge in general, and knowledge of good and evil in particular, are good for human beings. This has always been acknowledged as the greatest obstacle to regarding God's commandment not to eat the fruit as just. The point is too obvious to need detailed exposition, and besides it is set out in *Paradise Lost* in compelling terms, when the serpent advocates disobedience to Eve with consummate forensic skill.[3]

For all of these reasons, Daube's interpretation of the story must be essentially correct. It is not a story of human sin and just punishment by a just God; it is a story of a deceitful god who is jealous of human progress and visits the most terrible retribution

[3]   John Milton, *Paradise Lost*, 9.678ff.

on the man and woman who take the first perilous and defiant step towards civilized human life. It is the earliest affirmation in our culture of the value of knowledge for human beings, and its indispensible place in human life. This is not all the story is about. But it appears to be its main significance, what it was principally meant to teach.

§3 Several centuries after Genesis was written down, Plato presented a puzzle about the value of knowledge in the *Meno*. Plato was not a sceptic about the value of knowledge. He did not doubt that knowledge is the guide we really need, when we are deciding what to think or what to do. But he showed that once knowing is distinguished from merely having right opinion, it becomes difficult to say why. The advantage of knowledge over ignorance, which the author of Genesis was concerned with, is evident, and not hard to explain. But it not so obvious why knowledge is preferable to correct opinion:

> *Socrates*: If a man knew the way to Larissa, or any other place you please, and walked there and led others, would he not be a good guide?
> *Meno*: Certainly.
> *Socrates*: And a person who had the right opinion as to which was the way, but had never been there and did not really know, might also be a good guide, might he not?
> *Meno*: Certainly.
> *Socrates*: And presumably as long as he has the right opinion, he will be just as good a guide as the one who knows – if he believes the truth instead of knowing it.
> *Meno*: Just as good.
> *Socrates*: Hence true opinion is as good a guide to acting the right way as knowledge is . . . (Meno, 97a-c)

This is the puzzle. Knowing is not the same as happening to having the right opinion. For example, noone can know now which team will win the next World Cup. But all over the world there are people who firmly believe that their national team is going to win, and some of them will turn out to be right. They do not know their team is going to win, any more than the others know *their* teams are going to win. The difference is that their belief happens to be true. So knowing must be distinguished from merely having the right opinion, or believing something that

happens to be true. But once we have drawn this distinction, it becomes much harder to explain why we prize knowledge as highly as we do. Considered as a guide to action, true belief appears to be as valuable as knowledge, because the one who knows the truth and the one who merely believes the truth will offer the same advice. So why does it matter what we know?[4]
Here is Socrates' solution. Knowledge, he explains, is more valuable than mere true belief, because true beliefs are like the statues made by Daedalus,[5] which were so lifelike that they ran away unless they were tied down:

> So long as they stay with us, [true beliefs] are a fine possession, and effect all that is good; but they do not care to stay for long, and run away out of the human soul, and thus are of no great value until one ties them down by working out the cause [*aitias logismo*]. That process, my dear Meno, is recollection, as we agreed earlier. (Meno 97e-98a)

The interpretation of this passage is controversial, especially the phrase '*aitias logismo*', which I have translated as 'working out the cause'. However, Socrates appears to be saying that what makes a true belief more durable, more stable, is understanding why it is true; and he is certainly claiming that the stability of knowledge is what makes it more valuable than true belief:

> Once they are tied down, they become knowledge, and are stable. That is why knowledge is more valuable than true opinion. What distinguishes one from the other is the tether. (Meno, 98a)

---

[4]   Throughout this chapter I talk in general terms about the value of knowledge, but this should always be read as referring to the questions raised by this passage from the *Meno*: is true opinion as good a guide to acting the right way as knowledge? If not, why not? I do not mean to imply that knowledge is always preferable to ignorance, that the advance of science has benefits but no costs, or that every fact is worth knowing. Nor am I concerned, directly at least, with the value of the concept of knowledge, as opposed to the value of knowledge itself. These topics have not always been sharply distinguished (see, for example, Edward Craig, *Knowledge and the State of Nature* (Oxford: OUP 1990), pp. 2–8), but they are distinct.

[5]   Cf. *Euthyphro*, 11c. Plato may be making an ironic reference to the opening lines of Pindar, *Nemean* 5: 'I am not a sculptor, to make statues that stand motionless on their base. Sweet song, go on every merchant-ship and rowboat that leaves Aegina, and spread the news . . .'

In sum, Plato's idea appears to be that knowledge involves understanding why the things we know to be true are true; and that understanding this makes us able to hold fast to the truth, and avoid lapsing into falsehood. And that explains why knowledge is more valuable than true belief.[6]

§4 The solution is ingenious, but it is not convincing. In the first place, beliefs that do not have a rational foundation are not necessarily unstable. Some of our most stable beliefs are inculcated in us as children, without being tied down by 'working out the cause' – moral and religious beliefs, for example. The prophets and imams who offer to guide us on the road to salvation generally tell us that they know the way; but even they are mistaken, their beliefs tend to be stable, perhaps because the stabilizing effect can be achieved by merely believing that you have 'worked out the cause'.

Second, the stability of knowledge, and its status as knowledge, are not invariably due to evidence or rational support. Russell and Whitehead completed their proof of the proposition that $1 + 1 = 2$ on page 86 of volume two of *Principia Mathematica*, and perhaps this counts as 'working out the cause'. But it is doubtful whether the proof transformed a belief into knowledge, or made it more stable, and less liable to 'run away'.

Third, knowledge is not uniformly more stable than belief. Since we are forgetful, we lose a good deal of the knowledge we acquire – trivial knowledge, such as the number of coins I have in my pocket, much of the knowledge we acquire when we read a newspaper, and much of the knowledge we acquire at school. Some philosophers maintain that whether the beliefs we acquire by testimony – for example, when we read the papers – count as knowledge or mere opinion can depend on the reliability of the source. And that may be right. But the reliability of the source – as opposed to what we believe about it – will not normally affect how securely we hold on to these beliefs, or how easily they are forgotten, and slip out of our minds.

Fourth, as Edward Craig has pointed out, whether the stability of a person's beliefs is important depends on which beliefs we are considering, and the circumstances.

---

[6] I shall not discuss the doctrine of recollection, which Socrates refers to in this passage. See G. Vlastos, 'Anamnesis in the *Meno*', *Dialogue* 4 (1965) pp. 143–67, repr. in Jane M. Day, ed., *Plato's Meno in Focus* (Abingdon: Routledge, 1994).

Many beliefs are required for the guidance of single, 'one-off' actions under circumstances that will not recur, and once the particular occasion is past there is no obvious value at all in their persistence.[7]

For example, it is important for me to have a true belief now about the time I am due to meet a visitor this afternoon, and the time when I promised to call a friend in Los Angeles tonight. But by next Wednesday, it probably won't matter whether I have retained either of these beliefs.

§5 For these reasons, Plato's own solution to his problem is unconvincing, as it stands. And this may make us wonder whether the problem is real. *Is* knowledge more valuable than true belief? Perhaps the idea is an illusion. Perhaps it is part of the mystification of knowledge Wittgenstein criticized in *On Certainty* (§§6 & 12): '. . . a queer and extremely important mental state . . . a state of affairs which guarantees what is known, guarantees it as a fact.' Perhaps it is a nostalgic tribute to a conception of knowledge – Plato's, Descartes's – we do not share.[8]

Whatever one may think about these diagnoses, a sceptical attitude to Plato's problem – in other words, the thought that perhaps there is *no* advantage to possessing knowledge as opposed to true belief – has become quite widespread in the last forty years or so, since the publication of Gettier's article 'Is justified true belief knowledge?', for four main reasons.[9]

First, Gettier showed that justified true belief is not sufficient for knowledge, from which it follows that knowledge is not necessary for justified true belief. But in that case, why should we care about knowledge? Crispin Wright expresses this thought as follows:

> We can live with the concession that we do not, strictly, *know* some of the things we believed ourselves to know, provided we can retain the thought that we are fully justified in accepting them.[10]

---

[7]   Edward Craig, *op. cit.*, p. 7.
[8]   See, for example, Stephen Stich, *The Fragmentation of Reason* (Cambridge, Mass.: MIT Press, 1990), pp. 122f.; Jonathan L. Kvanvig, *The Value of Knowledge and the Pursuit of Understanding* (Cambridge: CUP, 2003), *passim*; Duncan Pritchard, *Knowledge* (Houndmills: Palgrave Macmillan, 2009), ch. 7.
[9]   See, for example, Jonathan Kvanvig, *op. cit.*, p. 139.
[10]   Crispin Wright, 'Scepticism and Dreaming: Imploding the Demon', *Mind* 100 (1991), p. 88.

Second, if we seek knowledge, and justified true belief is insufficient for knowledge, how can we seek the extra elusive element
knowledge requires? We can seek fresh evidence supporting the
hypothesis we favour, and test and interrogate the evidence we
believe we already have. But we could not seek the elusive ingre-
dient that distinguishes knowledge from justified true belief, even
if we could say exactly what it is. Mark Kaplan makes this point as
follows:

> All we can do by way of seeking knowledge is seek justified
> belief and hope that this justified belief will satisfy whatever
> other conditions a justified belief must satisfy in order to qualify
> as knowledge.[11]

It seems to follow that whatever the difference between knowledge and justified belief may be, scientific research, and rational
inquiry in general, can simply ignore it. It *can* ignore it, because it
must.

Third, many of the analyses of knowledge proposed during the
decades that followed the publication of Gettier's article made it
difficult to understand why knowledge should be more advanta-
geous or more valuable than true belief.

In some cases it is their sheer complexity. For example, Mar-
shall Swain proposed that:

S knows that p if and only if
  (1) p
  (2) S believes that p
  (3) there is a set of reasons, A, such that
     (a) S's belief that p is based on A,
     (b) S's believing that p on the basis of A is justified,
     (c) S has A as a result of at least one non-defective causal
         ancestry, and
     (d) if S has any other reasons, B, that are relevant to S's
         justifiably believing that p, then S would be justified
         in believing that p on the basis of $A \cup B$.

If this is what knowledge is, can it really matter? Should we care
whether someone actually knows something, because all three

[11] Mark Kaplan, 'It's Not What You Know That Counts', *Journal of Philosophy* 82 (1985),
p. 361.

conditions are satisfied, or merely has a justified true belief, because (3)(d) isn't satisfied? It is difficult to see why.

In other cases it is the specific content of the analysis that makes it hard to understand why knowledge matters. For example, Nozick's proposal (expressed in the jargon of possible worlds and simplified a little) is that:

S knows that p if and only if
  (1) p
  (2) S believes that p
  (3) in possible worlds close to the actual world, S believes that p if p is true, and S does not believe that p if p is false.

Knowledge, as Nozick put it, is belief that tracks the truth.

Now Nozick acknowledged that this analysis is unsatisfactory as it stands, because there are cases where S knows that p despite the fact that in some close possible worlds in which p is false, S still believes that p. So *these* non-actual worlds should not appear in (3). They don't have anything to do with the difference between knowledge and mere true belief. But suppose we succeeded in defining a set of possible worlds W that appeared to make the analysis watertight:

S knows that p if and only if
  (1) p
  (2) S believes that p
  (3) in W, S believes that p if p is true, and S does not believe that p if p is false.

If this were what knowledge is, it would be hard to see why knowledge is more valuable than true belief. It is obvious that I want my beliefs, and the beliefs of others I rely on – the guide who shows me the way to Larissa, for example – to be true in the actual world. But why does it matter whether my beliefs are true in possible but non-actual worlds? Why should I mind whether my journeys to Larissa in possible but non-actual worlds – the journeys I *could* take but *don't* take – end in the right place? For all I care, they can take me to Crawford, Texas or Guantanamo Bay.[12]

---

[12] A similar argument applies if we distinguish between close and distant possible worlds. For I am no worse off if I narrowly escape disaster than if I escape it by a wide

The fourth reason why epistemology post-Gettier has encouraged the thought that knowledge may not be more valuable than true belief is that most of the vast literature addressing Gettier's puzzle about knowledge sought to capture the idea that if we know the truth we do not believe the truth fortuitously or by luck. But benefits are not worth any less because they were gained fortuitously or by luck. We may admire a man less for winning the lottery than for inventing the bagless vacuum cleaner, but pound for pound their fortunes are worth the same.

§6 To summarize the main points covered so far: First, Plato's proposal is that 'Once [true beliefs] are tied down, they become knowledge, and are stable. That is why knowledge is more valuable than true opinion. What distinguishes one from the other is the tether.' But this is unconvincing for four reasons. (i) Beliefs that do not have a rational foundation are not necessarily unstable. (ii) The stability of knowledge is not invariably due to evidence or rational support. (iii) Knowledge is not uniformly more stable than belief. (iv) Whether the stability of a person's beliefs is important depends on which beliefs we are considering, and the circumstances.

Second, Gettier's article 'Is justified true belief knowledge?', and the literature it spawned, cast doubt on the idea that knowledge is more valuable than true belief, for four reasons. (i) If knowledge is not necessary for justified true belief, justification cannot be the reason why we should value knowledge more. (ii) We cannot seek knowledge as opposed to justified true belief; so whatever the factor is, which distinguishes between them, scientific research or rational enquiry can ignore it. (iii) Many of the definitions of knowledge devised to deal with Gettier-type cases made it hard to see why knowledge should be more valuable than true belief, either because of their complexity, or because of their specific content. (iv) Believing the truth fortuitously, or by luck, does not diminish the advantage it confers.

I should like to make one further observation about Gettier, before moving on. It is implicit in what I have already said about

margin, assuming I am not aware of my situation in either case. Cf. Edward Craig, *op. cit.*, p. 20. Linda Zagzebski argues, in a similar vein, that reliabilist theories of knowledge make it hard to understand why knowledge should be considered more valuable than mere true belief. See 'What is Knowledge', in J. Greco and E. Sosa, eds., *Epistemology* (Oxford: Blackwell, 1999), pp. 92–116.

the impact of his article; but it is worth making it explicit. As I said a moment ago, Gettier's article showed that justification cannot be the factor that makes knowledge more valuable than true belief.[13] But this makes Plato's puzzle more difficult to solve. Ever since Plato, it has not been enough to explain why knowledge is more valuable than ignorance. We need to need to explain why knowledge is more valuable than mere true belief. And since Gettier, it's no longer enough to explain why knowledge is more valuable than mere true belief. We now need to need to explain why knowledge is more valuable than *justified* true belief. It's as if the dialogue had changed, like this:

> *Socrates*: If a man knew the way to Larisa, or any other place you please, and walked there and led others, would he not be a good guide?
> *Meno*: Certainly.
> *Socrates*: And a person who had the right opinion *with a justification* as to which was the way, but had never been there and did not really know, might also be a good guide, might he not?
> *Meno*: Certainly.
> *Socrates*: And presumably as long as he has the right opinion *with a justification*, he will be just as good a guide as the one who knows – if he believes the truth instead of knowing it.
> *Meno*: Just as good.
> *Socrates*: Hence true opinion *with a justification* is as good a guide to acting the right way as knowledge is . . .

I do not mean to impy that Gettier moved the goalposts; but he raised the bar. And as we have seen, that makes it more tempting to duck the challenge, and deny that knowledge *is* more valuable than true belief.

§7 I want to return now to Plato's own solution to his puzzle, the idea that knowledge is more durable, more stable than true belief. I've explained why this solution is unsatisfactory, as it stands. But Timothy Williamson defends a qualified version of it in *Knowledge and its Limits*, which I shall consider now.

---

[13] Gettier implies that Plato thought justification was the factor that makes knowledge more valuable than true belief; but this is unlikely to be the right interpretation of the passage in *Meno*.

Williamson's immediate purpose in this passage is to argue that knowledge and belief have, as he puts it, different 'causal powers', so that explanations of behaviour referring to knowledge are not equivalent to ones referring to belief. Knowledge, Williamson explains, is less likely to be lost when new evidence comes to light than mere true belief:

> One can lose a mere true belief by discovering the falsity of further beliefs on which it had been essentially based; quite often, the truth will out. One cannot lose knowledge in that way, because a true belief essentially based on false beliefs does not constitute knowledge. For example, I might derive the true belief that this road goes to Larissa from the two false (but perhaps justified) beliefs that Larissa is due north and that this road goes due north; when dawn breaks in an unexpected quarter and I realize that this road goes south, without having been given any reason to doubt that Larissa is due north, I abandon the belief that this road goes to Larissa.[14]

It is true, of course, that some beliefs are adhered to dogmatically, whatever evidence comes to light. But Williamson claims that *if we are rational*, then knowledge is more durable than mere true belief:

> Present knowledge is less vulnerable than mere present true belief to *rational* undermining by future evidence . . . Other things being equal, given rational sensitivity to new evidence, present knowledge makes future true belief more likely than mere present true belief does.[15]

This is an ingenious elaboration of Plato's own solution to his puzzle, but I believe it fails, for three reasons.

First, on Williamson's account, as on Plato's, the advantage of knowledge over mere true belief varies depending on how probable it is that the belief concerned will be undermined by the discovery of another truth; and the greater value of knowledge is sometimes negligible (i.e. so small that it can be ignored) because the probability of discovering such a truth is sometimes negligible.

[14]   T. Williamson, *Knowledge and its Limits* (Oxford: OUP, 2000), p. 78.
[15]   *Ibid.*, p. 101.

Second, on Williamson's account, again like Plato's, the advantage of knowledge over true belief only concerns the future, because of course that is what durability is all about. So knowledge that doesn't have a shelf life is no more valuable, as a guide to acting the right way, than mere true belief. Williamson concedes this point, but he argues that it does not represent a shortcoming in his account:

> The present argument concerns only delayed impact, not action at the next 'instant'. We do not value knowledge more than true belief for instant gratification.[16]

But this is unconvincing. It is true that we do not value knowledge for instant gratification; but we do not value it for deferred gratification either. Knowledge is sometimes gratifying and sometimes painful, and the value we attach to it does not normally depend on which it is. Hence an account, like Plato's or Williamson's, which makes the advantage of knowledge over true belief contingent on what may happen in the future, remains open to the charge that it is unsatisfactory or incomplete.

One might respond to these two points, on Williamson's behalf, by denying that knowledge is more valuable than true belief regardless of the future, by accepting that the difference in value between knowledge and true belief may be vanishingly small, and by insisting that, if we are rational, knowledge is *normally* more durable than true belief. In other words, one might simply insist that this is the best that we can do, or that it is all that it makes sense to attempt.[17] But a third objection shows that even on these limited terms, Williamson's solution to Plato's puzzle fails.

§8 Williamson's solution is that if we are rational, knowledge is less likely to be undermined by future evidence than true belief: knowledge, as he puts it, is relatively robust. Here again is the example I mentioned earlier:

> I might derive the true belief that this road goes to Larissa from the two false (but perhaps justified) beliefs that Larissa is due

---

[16]   *Ibid.*, p. 79.
[17]   As a discussant at the *Ratio* conference pointed out, if someone claimed that marriage is more valuable than cohabitation because it is a more durable relationship, their argument would not be invalidated by pointing out that this is normally but not invariably the case.

north and that this road goes due north; when dawn breaks in an unexpected quarter and I realize that this road goes south, without having been given any reason to doubt that Larissa is due north, I abandon the belief that this road goes to Larissa.

But what does this example really show? Williamson takes it to support the claim that

> Present knowledge is less vulnerable than mere present true belief to rational undermining by future evidence.

But this is not quite right. The claim it really supports is that

> Present knowledge or mere present true belief whose justification does not include a falsehood (NFL, i.e. no false lemmas) is less vulnerable than present true belief whose justification does include a falsehood (FL) to rational undermining by future evidence.[18]

Williamson is right to say that 'a true belief essentially based on false beliefs does not constitute knowledge'. But a true belief *not* essentially based on false beliefs may not constitute knowledge either. So the example really supports the claim that *either* knowledge *or* mere true belief NFL is more valuable than true belief FL. But it does not support the claim that knowledge is more valuable than mere true belief *sans phrase*.

I stated this objection quite abruptly, so I shall present it again, in a slightly different way.

We have already seen that Gettier made Plato's puzzle more difficult to solve. He showed that it isn't enough to explain why knowledge is more valuable than true belief: we need to explain why knowledge is more valuable than *justified* true belief. As I put it earlier, he raised the bar. Then, when the post-Gettier industry got going, each time a more exacting set of conditions for knowledge was shown to be insufficient the bar was raised by another increment.

---

[18] In fact we need a further qualifying phrase: *as long as there is some chance that the falsehood will come to light*. There may be falsehoods that can never come to light. For example, Goldbach's conjecture, that every even number is the sum of two prime numbers, is true but unprovable, its contradictory is an undiscoverable falsehood.

One of the times this happened was in the early 1970s, when a number of philosophers pointed out that Gettier's counter-examples to the thesis that knowledge is justified true belief are cases where a falsehood fortuitously justifies a truth, and claimed, on the strength of that observation, that knowledge is true belief NFL. But counter-examples – that is, examples showing that true belief NFL is not sufficient for knowledge – sprung up in the literature like mushrooms, which meant that the new thesis about knowledge failed.[19]

But it also meant that Plato's puzzle became even more difficult to solve. Because it showed that it isn't even enough to explain why knowledge is more valuable than *justified* true belief: we need to explain why knowledge is more valuable than true belief NFL. As we have seen, Williamson's example sets knowledge on a par with true belief NFL. So of course it fails – that is, it fails to explain why it is better to know the road to Larissa than to have the right opinion, *whatever* kind of justification for the opinion we may have.[20]

Thus Williamson's and Plato's solutions fail for similar reasons. First, both imply that the advantage of knowledge over mere true belief depends on how likely it is that a truth which would undermine the belief will come to light. Second, neither solution explains why knowledge without a shelf life is more valuable than mere true belief. Third, Plato fails to explain why it is better to know than to have the right opinion, however stubborn the opinion is, whereas Williamson fails to explain why it is better to know than to have the right opinion, however free from the taint of falsehood the justification for the opinion is.

§9 Plato's puzzle about knowledge and true belief is surprisingly difficult to solve; and this makes it tempting to abandon the idea that knowledge is more valuable than true belief. The conviction that knowledge – fruit of the 'Sacred, Wise, and Wisdom-giving

---

[19] R. Feldman, 'An Alleged Defect in Gettier Counter-Examples', *Australasian Journal of Philosophy* 52 (1974), pp. 68–69; R.K. Shope, *The Analysis of Knowing* (Princeton N.J.: Princeton Univ. Press, 1983), chs. 1 & 2.

[20] The same argument applies *pari passu* if we compare knowledge with true belief that fails to qualify as knowledge because of the presence of counter-evidence (Williamson, *op. cit.*, pp. 78–79). Cases such as Goldman's story about barn façades only support the claim that present knowledge *or mere present true belief in the absence of counter-evidence* is less vulnerable than present true belief *in the presence of counter-evidence* to rational undermining by future evidence.

plant' – is a precious thing is an ineradicable part of human culture. But on our journeys to Larissa, and on our longer journeys to our various Ithacas, perhaps it is simply the truth that we value and desire, and it does not matter whether we attain the specially privileged relationship to it we call 'knowledge', as long as we are guided by the truth. In the remaining part of this chapter, I want to suggest, first, that what we care about, on the road to Larissa, is indeed being guided by the truth, no less and no more; and second, that this very fact about us explains why we prefer knowledge to true belief. So I shall try to reconcile the sceptical sentiment I conveyed a moment ago with Plato's conviction, that knowledge is a better guide to acting the right way than true belief, and do justice to both. If this is the right response to Plato's puzzle, the mistake made by sceptics about the value of knowledge (e.g. Kaplan, Kvanvig, Pritchard) and non-sceptics (e.g. Zagzebski, Sosa, Greco, Goldman & Olsson) alike is to force a choice that does not really exist.[21]

§10 The reason why Plato's own solution to his puzzle and Williamson's recent elaboration of it both fail is that the resources they deploy are too limited. In fact they are limited to two elements only: what I do, or shall do, or may do; and what I believe, or shall believe, or may believe. Only action and belief. And this is too limited a repertoire of concepts to explain why knowledge is a better guide to acting the right way than true belief. If we want to solve the puzzle, we need more. And to see exactly what is missing, we need think afresh about what knowledge is. I have written about this in the past, developing the idea, derived from Wittgenstein and Ryle, that knowledge – by which I mean propositional or factual knowledge – is an ability.[22]

[21] Sceptics: for citations see notes 8 and 11; non-sceptics: L. Zagzebski, 'The Search for the Source of Epistemic Good', Metaphilosophy, 34 (2003), pp. 12–28; J. Greco, 'Knowledge as Credit for True Belief', in M. DePaul & L. Zagzebski, eds., Intellectual Virtue: Perspectives from Ethics and Epistemology (Oxford: OUP, 2003); E. Sosa, A Virtue Epistemology: Apt Belief and Reflective Knowledge (Oxford: OUP, 2007), lecture 4; A.I. Goldman & E.J. Olsson, 'Reliabilism and the Value of Knowledge', in A. Haddock, A. Millar & D. Pritchard, eds., Epistemic Value (Oxford: OUP, 2009), pp. 19–41.
[22] 'How knowledge works', Philosophical Quarterly 49 (1999) pp. 433–451; 'Knowledge and Evidence', Mind 115 (2006), pp. 633–658. See also L. Wittgenstein, Philosophical Investigations (Oxford: Basil Blackwell, 1952), §150; G. Ryle, The Concept of Mind (London: Hutchinson, 1949), p. 129; A.R. White, The Nature of Knowledge (Totowa N.J.: Rowman and Littlefield, 1982), ch.5; A.J.P. Kenny, The Metaphysics of Mind (Oxford: OUP, 1989) p. 109. The idea that knowledge is an ability can be traced to Plato, Republic, 477d.

As soon as we think about knowledge in this way our conception of it is transformed, because instead of asking what we need to add to belief to get knowledge, or how knowledge differs from belief, we are forced to ask how knowledge gets exercised or expressed – since this is invariably how abilities are defined. And it turns out that it isn't difficult to say how knowledge gets exercised or expressed. For example, if I know that Larissa is due north, my knowledge gets exercised or expressed whenever the fact that Larissa is due north informs or guides the way I think or act – in other words, whenever it is one my reasons for modifying my thought or behaviour in some way.

The theory of knowledge I have defended is encapsulated in this example. The idea is simply that knowledge is the ability to be guided by the facts. The phrase 'guided by the facts' is a metaphor, of course, but it is a perfectly familiar one. When we talk about being guided by a fact, we mean that we took it into consideration, that it informed our reasoning, when we decided what to think or what to do. So the facts we are guided by are the facts that are our reasons.

Here is how we can arrive at this conception of knowledge in five steps:

(1) Factual knowledge is an ability.
(2) An ability is defined by what it is an ability to do (how it is exercised).
(3) Knowledge of a fact is exercised when the fact guides thought or action.
(4) A fact that guides thought or action is a fact that serves as a reason (for thinking or doing something).
(5) Factual knowledge is the ability to do things for reasons that are facts.

This is intended to explain, not to convince. I have tried to defend this way of thinking about knowledge in the earlier papers referred to above. And for present purposes, we only need to rely on part of it – specifically, on the idea that if a person does not know a certain fact, she is unable to do things for that reason. In other words, the fact that p cannot be a person's reason for doing something unless she knows that p. Hence it is not sufficient merely to have the true belief that p. If a person merely truly believes that p, the fact that p cannot be her reason for thinking something or for acting in a certain way.

One simple kind of case that illustrates this principle is where the fact in question is one that cannot be known. For example, it was impossible to know in 1997 which team would win the 1998 World Cup. But suppose Marianne had unshakeable faith in the French team and was perfectly convinced that France was going to win. And suppose she placed a bet of 1000 francs on France to win, for this reason. We know now that France *was* going to win, but we also know that Marianne did not know this when she placed her bet. So, what was her reason for placing the bet? If a fact cannot be person's reason if she merely has the corresponding true belief, the fact that France was going to win was not her reason. And this seems to be right. It seems clear that Marianne's reason for placing the bet was not the fact that France was going to win. Her reason was that she *believed*, or *was perfectly convinced*, that France would win.

If the claim I am relying on is true – if the fact that p cannot be a person's reason for doing something unless she knows that p – then if I believe, but do not know, that Larissa is due north, my reason for taking the road that leads north cannot be the fact that Larissa is due north, regardless of whether my belief is true. My reason may be that I believe that Larissa is due North, or that Larissa is probably due north, or that a sign indicates that Larissa is due north, or that someone told me that Larissa is due north. But the fact that Larissa is due north cannot be my reason, unless it is a fact I know. The relationship between knowledge and mere true belief is similar to the relationship between perception and veridical hallucination. The man who sees the guide take the road that leads due north, and follows him, is guided by the man he sees; whereas the man who hallucinates is not, even though he follows the same route.

§11 The claim that the fact that p cannot be a person's reason for doing something unless she knows that p provides a new solution to Plato's puzzle. For we do not only care about what we do, or want, or believe, we also care about our reasons, and in particular, we want our reasons to be facts. There is little reason to hope that we shall ever be guided by a pillar of cloud and a pillar of fire, like the children of Israel crossing the desert to the promised land. But we are sometimes guided by the facts. For example, if we know that the road that leads north is the road to Larissa, then we can take the road that leads north *because* it is the road to Larissa, whereas if we don't know this, we cannot. Hence, we are bound to regard knowledge as a better guide to acting the right way than mere true belief, because we care whether we are guided by the facts.

I said earlier that I want to reconcile the conviction that knowledge is more valuable than mere true belief with the sceptical thought that all we care about is being guided by the truth, and it does not matter whether we attain the privileged relationship to it we call 'knowledge' or not. The solution is simple. True belief, whether justified or not, will tend to influence thought and behaviour in the same way as knowledge does. So the man who has the right opinion about the way to Larissa – the man who believes that Larissa is due north, but has never been there and does not really know – will lead us in the right direction, as Socrates points out. It follows that if all we cared about was getting to Larissa, we would not, or at any rate, should not prefer knowledge to mere true belief. But only the person who knows will be guided by the fact that Larissa is due north – and not merely influenced by his state of mind. Since we care about being guided by the truth, we are bound to regard knowledge as a better guide to acting the right way than mere true belief.

But why do we care about being guided by the truth? Suppose we say that a person who merely believes that p, and uses the proposition that p as a premise, is 'as if guided by p'. Why do we prefer to be guided by the truth rather than to be merely as if guided by the truth? As Hume put it, these questions seem to throw us back into the same uncertainty, from which we have endeavoured to extricate ourselves.

But in fact it isn't the same uncertainty at all. The question is interesting. But it is different from the question we began with, and it has a different answer.

Q1: Why do we prefer knowledge as a guide to action rather than true belief?
A: Because we prefer to be guided by the truth.
Q2: Why do we prefer to be guided by the truth rather than to be as if guided by the truth?

Various answers to this question are possible. One is that we prefer reality to illusion. Another is that we prefer not to be deceived about what our reasons are. To expand on these answers in a satisfying way would take up a good deal more space, particularly because they raise further difficult questions of their own. So there is, as there always is, more to say. But I believe we have made some progress if we have shown that our conviction that knowledge is more valuable than true belief is consistent with the sceptical thought that all we care about is being guided by the truth; and if we have shown that a plausible solution to Plato's puzzle will have to step beyond the question of what we do and what we believe, to the question of our reasons.

4

WHAT IS THE CONTENT OF AN INTENTION IN ACTION?

John McDowell

Abstract
On the view proposed, the content of an intention in action is
given by what one would say in expressing it, and the proper form
for expressing such an intention is a statement about what one is
doing: e.g. 'I am doing such-and-such'. By contrast, some think that
there are normative or evaluative elements to the content of an
intention in action which would be left out of a form that merely
stated facts. They think that the appropriate way to express such an
intention is a statement about what one should be doing. Davidson,
for example, thinks that the statement must essentially be a verdict:
that doing such-and-such is all-out desirable. But this is to assume
that practical reason is reasoning towards the truth of a proposition, the very mistake which obscures its 'true character', as
Anscombe correctly points out. Moreover, although Davidson's
view helps him account for the possibility of weakness of will, his
explanation of the phenomenon is strained and inferior by contrast with the account which the proposed view makes available.
The proposed view fits into a broader picture in which intentional
action is the exercise of a practical conceptual capacity.

1. Robert Brandom suggests intentions in action should be
understood as *volitions*, in a sense Wilfrid Sellars attaches to that
term.[1]

Sellars explains volitions as what intentions for the future
become when the time for acting comes. I think some intentions
in action can be described in just those terms: they started out as
intentions for the future, and they have matured into intentions
in action. That is what happens with intentions for the future
when their time comes, provided that the subject realizes the time
for acting has arrived, and does not change her mind, and is not
prevented from acting. To that extent Brandom's proposal looks

---

[1] *Making It Explicit* (Cambridge, Mass.: Harvard University Press, 1994), pp. 256–9. See
Sellars's 'Thought and Action', in Keith Lehrer, ed., *Freedom and Determinism* (New York:
Random House, 1966), especially at p. 110 (cited by Brandom at *Making It Explicit*, 258).

Agents and Their Actions, First Edition. Edited by Maximilian de Gaynesford. © 2011 Blackwell
Publishing Ltd. Published 2011 by Blackwell Publishing Ltd.

promising, though it would need to be adjusted to accommodate doing things intentionally on the spur of the moment, where there are intentions in action that did not start out as intentions for the future.

But there is a more pressing problem for the proposal, and this will lead into an answer to my question.

Sellars frames his account of volitions in terms of a scenario in which an intention for the future, expressible by saying 'I shall raise my hand in ten minutes', becomes, after ten minutes, a volition, expressible by saying 'I shall raise my hand now'. At that point Sellars's subject, Jones, starts to raise his hand.

In this scenario 'now', in 'I shall raise my hand now', refers to the moment at which an intention for the future matures into an intention in action. We might say 'I shall raise my hand now' signals the *onset* of an intention in action. But until Jones gets to the end of saying 'I shall raise my hand now', the period during which the intention is going to be in action is still in the future; it starts only when he says 'now' and begins to raise his hand. Sellars's policy with 'shall' is to detach it from its usual role as an auxiliary yielding a future tense, and appropriate it for expressing intentions in general, not necessarily for the future. But even raising one's hand takes time, and that prevents 'now', in Sellars's expression for a volition, from completely undoing the connection between 'shall' and futurity. The relevant hand-raising is only beginning at the moment at which Jones utters 'now' and starts to raise his hand. But the intention to raise his hand will be in action throughout the time it takes to raise his hand.

That suggests that the appropriate form for expressing an intention in action might be exemplified not by 'I shall raise my hand now', which one might say as one starts to raise one's hand, but by 'I am raising my hand', which one can say at any time during the relevant hand-raising.

Of course not just any utterance of 'I am crossing the street' would express an intention. (I have moved to a different example, for a reason I shall give in a moment.) I might say 'I am crossing the street' while I am being wheeled around in a wheelchair or swept along by a flood. A street-crossing I am in the midst of need not be intentional on my part.

I have changed Sellars's example because it is harder to imagine a case in which 'I am raising my hand' would not express an intention. If my hand's going up is not intentional on my part, it is natural to say 'My hand is rising' rather than 'I am raising my hand'. But that is special to actions described in terms of bodily performances a typical agent can immediately engage in. Something similar would go for 'I am *walking* across the street'. But there are verbs or verb phrases that are like 'cross the street' in that they can characterize intentional action but need not. And with them we need a distinction between two uses of the progressive present in the first person: one that expresses intentions and one that does not.

The key to the difference is that in the case in which I am being wheeled about I would need *observation* to be entitled to say 'I am crossing the street'. When one knows something observationally, things are as one takes them to be independently of one's taking them to be that way. One's taking them to be that way is an exercise of a receptive capacity. But if I express an intention in saying 'I am crossing the street', and I am indeed crossing the street, my utterance is a statement of knowledge that is not derived from the fact known, and in fact knowledge that is practical, in the sense G. E. M. Anscombe borrows from Aquinas.[2]

Here is a suggestion, then. The content of an intention in action is given by what one would say in expressing it, or what one would say in stating the practical knowledge one has in executing it, which comes to the same thing. And the appropriate form is 'I am doing such-and-such'.

2. I have put practical knowledge in place in terms of a quite abstract contrast with knowledge derived from the fact known. Much more would need to be said about the contrast. And I shall not do much of what is needed here. I am going to approach the topic obliquely, by considering a threat from a different direction – unlike Sellars's play with 'shall' – to the idea that the proper form of expression for intentions in action is 'I am doing such-and-such'.

A statement of that form is a statement of purported fact. That is so even if any knowledge the statement purports to state is practical knowledge. The opposing thought I want to consider is that a merely fact-stating form cannot express an intention; that would require a normative or evaluative element.

---

[2] See *Intention* (Oxford: Blackwell, 1957; reissued Cambridge, Mass.: Harvard University Press, 2000), p. 82 and following.

In his essay 'Intending',[3] Donald Davidson proposes that intentions, whether in action or for the future, are appropriately expressed by statements to the effect that doing such-and-such is all-out desirable.[4] I shall take Davidson's proposal as an exemplar of the opposing thought I have just introduced.

The point of 'all-out' is to make a contrast with statements of prima facie desirability, statements to the effect that something is desirable *in so far as* it has such-and-such a feature. Something may be desirable in so far as it has one feature but undesirable in so far as it has another. Eating a steak may be desirable in so far as it will taste delicious, but undesirable in so far as it will promote clogging of one's arteries. A prima facie statement of desirability gives, in its 'in so far as . . .' clause, something that can be said in favour of its topic, and is consistent with the possibility that there is also something to be said against it, and indeed that the case against it is more telling than the case for it.

What Davidson wants in an expression of intention, in contrast, is an outright *verdict* in favour of acting in a certain way.

In Davidson's essay 'How is weakness of the will possible?',[5] there is a version of this idea with an extra twist. This will help to bring out the significance of the contrast between prima facie and all-out statements. The extra twist is to accommodate the fact that it may be intentional on someone's part that she is doing one thing *as opposed to another.* A weak-willed person does B intentionally though she thinks it would be better to do A. What she does intentionally is: B rather than A. The scope of the specification of her intention includes the phrase introduced by 'rather than . . .'. And here Davidson's doctrine takes this form: the content of an intention of this sort is expressible by an all-out comparative evaluation, an all-out statement that the action undertaken is preferable to the action not undertaken.

As before, what it is for a statement to have the all-out form is that it is not conditional on this or that consideration about its subject matter. The content is not that doing this is better than doing that in so far as . . . , but that doing this is better than doing that, period.

---

[3]   In *Essays on Actions and Events* (Oxford: Clarendon Press, 1980).
[4]   Davidson identifies intentions with all-out judgments of desirability (p. 99). But he resists putting any weight on the term 'judgment' (p. 97, n. 7). His thinking seems well captured in terms of forms of words that express intentions.
[5]   Also in *Essays on Actions and Events.*

Davidson insists that these forms – all-out judgments of preferability and judgments of preferability in so far as . . . – are distinct even if the 'in so far as . . .' clause includes everything the subject takes to be relevant to the question which of the two courses of action is preferable. In that case the judgment is an all things considered judgment. An all things considered judgment that one course is preferable to another is still a prima facie judgment, still a judgment of preferability in so far as . . . , even though what fills the blank includes everything the subject thinks relevant. Like any prima facie judgment, such a judgment is logically distinct from an all-out verdict. A weak-willed person judges a course of action she does not follow better all things considered than a course of action she does follow, but she intentionally does what she does rather than the alternative. In Davidson's account that is to say she combines an all things considered judgment in favour of the course she does not take with an all-out judgment in favour of the course she does take.

Of course that implies a defect in rationality. If she thinks A is more strongly supported than B by the totality of the considerations she takes to be relevant to the question which is better, it is irrational for her to judge all-out that B is better than A. And this implication of irrationality is just what Davidson wants. The point of invoking the contrast between judgments all-out and judgments all things considered is not to make the weak-willed person look perfectly rational, but to enable *us* to avoid contradiction when we describe her. Davidson's doctrine about intention requires us to say she judges that acting as she does is better than the alternative. Since she acts against her better judgment, we have to say also that she does not judge that acting as she does is better than the alternative. That can make it seem that we are stuck in a contradiction. But our description is free of inconsistency if we say she judges all-out in favour of acting as she does and does not judge all things considered in favour of acting as she does. It is not the same judgment that according to our description she both makes and does not make.

Nothing hangs on Davidson's choice of 'desirable', or, for comparative judgments, 'better than' or 'preferable to', in these proposed forms for expressing intentions. His point turns on the distinction between all-out and prima facie judgments, rather than the specific content of the pairs of judgments that exemplify that distinction. It is not even crucial to his thinking to align intentions with judgments that are in a narrow sense *evaluative*. At one point in 'Intending' he considers a subject with an intention to improve the taste of a stew, who moves from there, by reasoning, to an intention to add sage. Davidson says the premise in this subject's reasoning that corresponds to the intention it starts from should be 'evaluative in form' (p. 86). But it becomes clear that he means 'evaluative' in a very general sense, not one that contrasts with, say, 'deontic' or 'normative', when he goes on to propose, as forms of words that would be suitable to capture this intention, both 'It is desirable to improve the taste of the stew' and 'I ought to improve the taste of the stew'. For him nothing evidently turns on any difference between these.

3. Davidson formulates his doctrine that intentions are all-out judgments of desirability in a context in which he is endorsing the idea that an intention can be the conclusion of a bit of practical reasoning. And he thinks the doctrine is consistent with whatever is right about the Aristotelian thesis that drawing the conclusion of a bit of practical reasoning is acting, at least if the reasoning is for the here and now. The implication is that, as specifications of what one does when one draws a conclusion from a bit of practical reasoning, 'judging that doing such-and-such is all-out desirable' and 'intentionally doing such-and-such' are interchangeable.

Davidson's writings about action are full of admiring invocations of Anscombe's *Intention*. There is one in the very section of 'Intending' in which he puts forward the doctrine I am considering (p. 97, n. 6).

But at the beginning of her discussion of practical reasoning there, in a passage Davidson never mentions, Anscombe says this (pp. 57–8):

> 'Practical reasoning', or 'practical syllogism', which means the same thing, was one of Aristotle's best discoveries. But its true character has been obscured. It is commonly supposed to be ordinary reasoning leading to such a conclusion as: 'I ought to do such-and-such.' By 'ordinary reasoning' I mean the only reasoning ordinarily considered in philosophy: reasoning towards the truth of a proposition, which is supposedly shewn to be true by the premises.

She goes on to consider a supposed example of practical reasoning, on this view of it, in which the showing to be true is proof and the conclusion, supposedly entailed by the premises, is 'I ought to give this man some money'.

Now no doubt the reasoning Davidson envisages will typically not purport to *prove* its conclusion. (In some cases perhaps it may. Suppose the only available way to improve the taste of the stew is to add sage.) But, though Anscombe spends some time objecting to the idea of practical syllogisms as, specifically, proofs of propositional conclusions, I do not believe one can accommodate her point by envisaging premises that do no more than make it rational to accept that one ought to do such-and-such – or, she might have added, that doing such-and-such is all-out desirable – without amounting to a proof of the conclusion. Anscombe says we obscure Aristotle's discovery if we take practical reasoning to be reasoning towards the truth of a proposition. No doubt the conclusion that one ought to give the man money, or that giving him money is all-out desirable, is in some sense practical. (I shall come back to this later.) Even so, reasoning that persuades one *that those things are so* is reasoning towards the truth of those propositions. So by Anscombe's lights it is not practical reasoning at all. But that is just how Davidson fits his account of intentions into what is supposed to be an account of practical reasoning.

So Davidson's picture of intentions, which is designed to capture the thought that intentions can be conclusions of practical reasoning, flies in the face of what, according to Anscombe, is the first thing we need to register if we are to get practical reasoning – one of Aristotle's best discoveries – into our thinking at all. And it is not that Davidson argues against this claim of Anscombe's. It is as if he simply does not notice it.

4. Anscombe does not directly connect her contrasting account of practical reasoning with the question I am organizing things around, the question how intentions in action might be expressed.

She constructs a counterpart to the dietary practical syllogisms that figure in Aristotle, with the following premises (p. 60):

Vitamin X is good for all men over 60.
Pig's tripes are full of vitamin X.
I'm a man over 60.
Here's some pig's tripes.

And she goes on (pp. 60–1):

Aristotle seldom states the conclusion of a practical syllogism, and sometimes speaks of it as an action; so we may suppose the man who has been thinking on these lines to take some of the dish that he sees. But there is of course no objection to inventing a form of words by which he *accompanies* this action, which we may call the conclusion in a verbalised form. We may render it as:

> (*a*) So I'll have some
> or (*b*) So I'd better have some
> or (*c*) So it'd be a good thing for me to have some.

One might be tempted to find an opening for Davidson in the second and third of these. But we should begin with the first.

'So I'll do such-and-such' is a natural form for expressing *practical assent* – saying 'Yes' to an action – as one embarks on the action. Anscombe might have spoken of a form of words by which the agent accompanies *beginning* to act. The point here is of a piece with my claim that Sellars's form for expressions of volition is apt for signalling the onset of an intention in action, but not for expressing intentions in action in general. Drawing the conclusion of a bit of practical reasoning is something one does at a determinate moment. If the reasoning is for the here and now, drawing the conclusion is embarking on an action; that is the Aristotelian doctrine. To bring the action to completion, one needs to sustain the intention that begins to be in action at that time, over a period during which, if it was as a result of reasoning that one started to act, the reasoning, including whatever move is appropriately conceived as drawing a conclusion from it, is receding into the past. *Going on* intentionally doing something cannot be equated with drawing a conclusion from some practical reasoning, any more than going on believing something can be equated with drawing a conclusion from some theoretical reasoning, even if the way one came to believe it was by considering the premises of the reasoning and drawing the conclusion. So it is right that a form of words that is a verbal expression of drawing the conclusion should be suitable for expressing the onset of an intention in action rather than its continuation. And Anscombe's choice of words here – 'So I'll have some' – does not speak to the question what might be an appropriate expression for an intention in action while it is in action. The intention that is in action in one's having (eating) some pig's tripes – something that takes time – could hardly be expressed by saying 'I'll have some' as one is chewing one's third or fourth mouthful, and Anscombe cannot mean to suggest anything to the contrary.

This carries over to the second and third of her forms, the ones that superficially suggest a match with Davidson. 'So I'd better have some' and 'So it'd be a good thing for me to have some' are natural expressions for the same thing that is naturally expressed by 'So I'll have some': the initial undertaking of practical assent to having some pig's tripes, with the evaluative elements – 'I'd better', 'a good thing' – emphasizing that the assent is made in rational response to the reasoning. The syllogism supplies a reason for having some pig's tripes, and it is just another way of saying that to say that it reveals a respect in which having some pig's tripes is good by the agent's lights. But the conclusion of the reasoning is having some pig's tripes, not judging that it would be good to have some pig's tripes. There is no support here for Davidson's idea that the relevant intention in action, which would have to be a *continuing* assent to the action in which it is, is well expressed by a statement that taking some pig's tripes is all-out desirable, or all-out preferable to any alternative, with Anscombe's premises supposedly making it rational to hold that that is how things are.

Those remarks of Anscombe's are not the place to look for clues to an Anscombean view about how intentions in action, as opposed to onsets of intentions in action, might be expressed.

For that we should look earlier in *Intention*, where she considers a line of thought she says she was formerly tempted to encapsulate in the slogan 'I *do* what *happens*' (p. 52). By the time of writing *Intention*, she is resisting the temptation, but not abandoning the line of thought that the slogan was designed to capture.

The point of the slogan was that the knowledge of an action one has as its agent is knowledge of something that is happening, which is (in general) a kind of thing that can be known observationally. Anscombe brings practical knowledge into the picture to avert a mystery she says there would otherwise be about how there can be 'two knowledges – one by observation, the other in intention –' (p. 57) of the very same thing. If we do not recognize that knowledge in intention is not contemplative, we shall be induced to look for 'the different *mode of contemplative knowledge* in acting, as if there were a very queer and special sort of seeing eye in the middle of the acting' (ibid.). This is the point at which she turns to her discussion of practical reasoning, which starts with the remark about how Aristotle's discovery is obscured by a common prejudice about reasoning. We need to understand practical reasoning, she says, in order to understand practical knowledge. And she returns to practical knowledge at the end of her treatment of practical reasoning.

I think Anscombe's worry about the two knowledges concerns the relation between practical knowledge of an action and observational knowledge *on the agent's part* of the happening that the action is. But the happening is an element in the public world. It is observationally knowable by others too, if they have a suitable point of vantage on it.

If the content of an intention in action would be the content of a bit of practical knowledge, conceived in accordance with the thought encapsulated in the slogan 'I *do* what *happens*', then the content of my intention in, say, crossing the street would be expressed by a first-person counterpart of a statement that could be knowledgeably made – of course not in the first person – by someone else on the basis of observing the happening that is my doing what I am doing. An observer would say 'He is crossing the street'. So if my expression of intention expresses practical knowledge of that happening, the appropriate form is, just as I have been urging, 'I am crossing the street'.

5. So far all I have presented is a clash of authorities. Is there anything better than an argument from authority against Davidson's view?

As I said, Davidson seems not to notice the passage in Anscombe that threatens his thinking, let alone argue against it. The case he mounts for his account of intentions presupposes, already contrary to what I have found in Anscombe, that the content of the conclusion of a bit of practical reasoning is captured by a judgment of desirability. What he takes himself to need to argue is just that the judgment must be all-out rather than prima facie. But something he says in arguing for that may be helpful in adjudicating the implicit dispute between him and Anscombe.

Davidson writes ('Intending', pp. 98–9):

Prima facie judgements cannot be directly associated with actions, for it is not reasonable to perform an action merely because it has a desirable characteristic. It is a reason for acting that the action is believed to have a desirable characteristic, but the fact that the action is performed represents a further judgement that the desirable characteristic was enough to act on – that other considerations did not outweigh it. . . . The reasons that determine the description under which an action is intended do not allow us to *deduce* that the action is simply worth performing; all we can deduce is that the action has a feature that argues in its favour. This is enough, however, to allow us to give the intention with which the action was performed. What is misleading is that the reasons that enter this account do not generally constitute all the reasons the agent considered in acting, and so knowing the intention with which someone acted does not allow us to reconstruct his actual reasoning. For we may not know how the agent got from his desires and other attitudes – his prima facie reasons – to the conclusion that a certain action was desirable.

Consider Anscombe's practical syllogism that issues in a man's taking some pig's tripes. The premises display a feature that argues in favour of his doing that. If we know that the syllogism answers the question why he is doing that, we are thereby enabled to give the intention with which he is acting, in the way Davidson here envisages: his intention is to ingest some vitamin X by eating some pig's tripes.

Someone who takes some pig's tripes to get some vitamin X into him may or may not have considered other things that bear on the question whether to do that, perhaps that the pig's tripes will probably taste disgusting. Surely silence about this does not make Anscombe's syllogism somehow incomplete, as Davidson implies. Suppose we ask the man why he took the pig's tripes, and he gives us the premises of Anscombe's syllogism in response. Would we object that the explanation is incomplete until we know whether he considered the prospect of a disgusting taste and decided not to let it deter him? Anscombe's syllogism provides a reason-revealing explanation of his action, even if we think it was stupid of him not to be deterred by the prospect of a disgusting taste. Contrary to what Davidson says, it *can* be reasonable to perform an action merely because it has a desirable characteristic.

Suppose we know someone has taken some pig's tripes for the reason given by Anscombe's syllogism. In that case we know he judged the desirable characteristic spelled out in the syllogism's premises to be enough to act on. We know, for instance, that if he did consider the prospect of a disgusting taste, it did not deflect him from taking the pig's tripes. But saying he judged the desirable characteristic to be enough to act on is just another way of saying he made it his reason for acting – he took the pig's tripes for that reason.

Davidson says this judgment, that the desirable characteristic is enough to act on, is a further judgment represented by the fact that the action is performed. That wording – 'represented by the fact that the action is performed' – might fit what I have just said, but Davidson's picture seems to be different. His picture seems to be, not that attributing the further judgment is just another way of saying the person draws the conclusion, but that the further judgment is needed for the transition from the premises to the conclusion to be rational. Without this further judgment the premises yield only that there is something to be said for acting in the way in question, not an outright verdict in favour of acting in that way. Davidson would have to acknowledge that to know the man judged the desirable characteristic to be enough to act on is not yet to know what, if any, other things he took into account and judged to be outweighed by it; it is not yet to be in a position to reconstruct his actual reasoning, as Davidson conceives that. But as Davidson sees things, it is to know this: if the man did consider any considerations that pointed in other directions, he judged the desirable characteristic to outweigh them. Hence it is to know at least schematically how he got from his prima facie reasons to his conclusion, in a bit of practical reasoning as Davidson conceives that.

But here Davidson's idea that the conclusion must be an outright verdict in favour of doing such-and-such seems to be distorting the point of saying the agent judges the desirable characteristic to be enough to act on. As I said, the point is just to register that the agent draws the conclusion. What that means is not that he moves from a prima facie reason for acting as he does to an outright judgment in favour of doing that, but just that he acts as he does for the reason constituted by the desirable characteristic.

I can bring out the significance of the divergence I am urging by noting that it makes room for a picture of weak-willed action that differs from Davidson's, and seems superior to it.

A weak-willed person acts for a reason that she takes to tell less compellingly in favour of doing what she does than she takes some other reason to tell in favour of doing something else. By acting for that reason, she reveals that she takes it to be enough to act on. As before, saying this is just registering that she acts for that reason. She is irrational in that she acts for a reason that, by her own lights, is not as good a reason for doing what she does as another reason she has is for doing something else.

In the passage I have quoted, Davidson identifies judging that a certain desirable characteristic is enough to act on with judging that other considerations do not outweigh it. This belongs with his view that a weak-willed person judges acting as she does all-out preferable to an alternative that she judges preferable all things considered. But in the sense in which it is correct to say that a weak-willed person, like anyone who acts for a reason, judges the reason for which she acts to be enough to act on, that judgment is not to be equated with judging that the reason for which she acts is not outweighed by other considerations. The irrationality of the weak-willed person lies precisely in the fact that she judges that the reason for which she acts *is* outweighed by other considerations, even while, in acting as she does, she treats it as enough to act on. There is no need to strain, as Davidson does, to find a sense in which she judges her weak-willed action preferable to the course, better supported by reasons in her own view, that she does not take.

6. As I acknowledged, judgments of the sort that figure as conclusions in the kind of reasoning Anscombe says modern philosophers misidentify as practical reasoning are in some sense practical. That is true about the judgment 'I ought to give this man money' in the case she considers. And it is true about Davidson's candidate, the all-out judgment that giving the man money would be desirable.

Anscombe's view implies that practicality in the conclusion, in whatever sense it is in which these judgments are practical, makes no difference to the fact that reasoning that issues in these judgments is not practical reasoning, because it is reasoning towards the truth of the propositions that constitute the content of these judgments. Davidson's conception of intentions is designed to capture the idea that intentions can be conclusions of practical reasoning. So, as I have been urging, his conception of intentions reflects the blind spot for what practical reasoning really is that Anscombe finds in modern philosophy.

But if the judgments Davidson equates with intentions are practical in some sense, one might wonder whether it really is a blind spot. How could reasoning that issues in judgments that are practical not be practical reasoning?

I think the sense in which those judgments are practical is this: a judgment that giving this man money would be desirable, or, in the formulation Anscombe considers, that one ought to give this man money, stands to one's giving him money in a relation analogous to that in which an order stands to someone's obeying it. If an order is not independently objectionable, perhaps as lacking authority or impossible to obey, and is not obeyed, the defect is not in the order but in the disobedient conduct, whereas if things are not as one says they are in a purportedly factual statement, the defect is in the saying rather than in how things are. Similarly, if one does not act as one thinks one ought to act, the defect revealed by the mismatch is in the acting, not the judgment. The judgment may be defective, but it is not shown to be defective by the mismatch with what one does.

This contrast, which later philosophers have described in terms of opposed directions of fit, is drawn in the famous shopping-list passage in *Intention* (p. 56). Anscombe distinguishes the relations in which what a man buys stands to a list given him by his wife, which is a sort of order, and to a list made by a detective following him, which is a record of what he buys. Abstracting from the possibility that the order may be independently open to criticism – for instance, if one puts 'tackle for catching sharks' on a list of things to buy in Oxford – we can say that if the list and what the man buys do not match, then in the case of the order the defect is in what he does, and in the case of the record the defect is in the list.

When Anscombe draws this contrast, she is working up to her separation of practical knowledge from contemplative knowledge. And the distinction of locations for the defect in cases of mismatch is helpful in guiding us in that direction. An analogy between intentions and orders prepares us for appreciating how practical knowledge, knowledge in intention, differs from contemplative knowledge in that, so far from being derived from what is known, it is, in the phrase Anscombe takes from Aquinas, 'the cause of what it understands' (*Intention*, p. 87).

And I have acknowledged that there is an analogy between orders and statements of desirability. So is there reason here to agree with Davidson, after all, that a form of words suitable to capture the content of an intention should have the sort of practicality exemplified by statements of desirability? If we said 'Yes', we would be taking it that Anscombe is wrong about the blind spot. And we would have to give up the idea that the content of an intention just is the content of one's knowledge of what one is doing when one is executing it.

But the argument limps, and this last implication of it brings out how. It is precisely that knowledge that Anscombe says is not derived from what is known. If one is not doing what one says one is doing when one gives expression to a putative bit of practical knowledge, the *primary* defect is in what one is doing, not in what one says. But what one knows when one has a bit of practical knowledge is simply that one is doing such-and-such. There is no normative or evaluative element in the content of the knowledge, even though this knowledge is 'the cause of what it understands'.

What goes missing in the defence of Davidson that I am considering is this: the practicality of practical knowledge is compatible with, and indeed requires, the possibility of a *derivative* defect not in what one is doing but in what one says, if one expresses what purports to be a bit of practical knowledge when one is not doing the thing in question, or if one expresses the corresponding intention. (We can still say those come to the same thing.) If I express an intention in action by saying 'I am crossing the street', it is not by virtue of something that is so anyway, independently of the intention I express, that I am stating a bit of knowledge, if I am. If it were not for the intention, there would not be the relevant fact. But even so, if I am not crossing the street what I say is false in the ordinary way; things are not as I say they are.

At one point in *Intention* Anscombe comes close, at least, to obscuring this. She considers a case in which she is writing 'I am a fool' on a blackboard with her eyes shut, knowing in intention that she is doing that. And she says (p. 82):

Orders, however, can be disobeyed, and intentions fail to get executed. That intention for example would not have been executed if something had gone wrong with the chalk or the surface, so that the words did not appear. And my knowledge would have been the same even if this had happened. If then my knowledge is independent of what actually happens, how can it be knowledge of what does happen? Someone might say that it was a funny sort of knowledge that was still knowledge even though what it was knowledge of was not the case! On the other hand Theophrastus' remark holds good: 'the mistake is in the performance, not in the judgment'.

Citing the remark attributed to Theophrastus is insisting on the point I made by saying that the primary defect is in what she does rather than in what she says. By citing the remark in this context,

Anscombe can seem to imply that the other location for a defect, the one characteristic of statements, is irrelevant to this kind of knowledge – as if practical knowledge is indeed a funny sort of knowledge, still knowledge even if what it is knowledge of is not the case.

But it is surely wrong to suppose Anscombe's claim to be writing 'I am a fool' on the blackboard can express *knowledge* if those words are not getting written on the blackboard.[6]

Whatever Anscombe's point is in this passage, she cannot mean to be suggesting, in her own voice, that practical knowledge is indifferent to whether one is actually doing what one takes oneself to be doing. She came up with the slogan 'I *do* what *happens*', which paves the way for her introduction of practical knowledge, precisely in opposition to the temptation to interiorize what is known in intention so that it does not include what is actually happening, except perhaps for bodily movements (pp. 51–3). She cannot herself be falling into a version of that temptation here.

I am not sure what to make of this passage in Anscombe. Perhaps the problematic remarks are meant to be heard as spoken by an interlocutor, rather than by Anscombe herself.[7] And there may be other options for interpreting the passage. I am not going to offer a reading of it here. All I want to say about it is that we should not allow it to contradict the opposition to interiorizing what is known in intention that drives Anscombe's discussion of practical knowledge. We should insist that there is *knowledge* in intention only if what is happening is what one says is happening when one says what one is doing. If it is to express practical *knowledge*, the saying needs to be true in the ordinary way.

This undercuts the motivation I have been considering for the idea that an expression of intention in action should be something other than a statement of what one is doing, as in the Davidsonian view I have been resisting.[8]

---

[6]   It is not to the point to say that writing those words on the blackboard might be something one is doing even if one's current efforts at getting them written are not succeeding; when one realizes that the words are not appearing on the blackboard, one will try again. That is true, but what Anscombe claims to be doing is writing those words *with her eyes shut*. If, when she looks, the words turn out not to have appeared on the blackboard, she will not have been doing what she said she was doing.

[7]   Eylem Özaltun has a detailed reading on these lines.

[8]   'But an intention is a commitment, so surely it needs to be expressed in deontic or normative terms.' – A claim is a commitment, but claims need to be expressed in deontic terms only if they are claims about deontic or normative matters.

7. What Anscombe, or her interlocutor voice, seems to say, in that problematic passage, is that her practical knowledge, her knowledge in intention, would have been the same even if she had not been doing what she took herself to be doing. That looks like a *highest common factor* conception of knowledge in intention, according to which her knowledge in intention in the case she considers cannot extend further into objective reality, so to speak, than something that would not be falsified if, say, the chalk were not working. One might make this concrete by saying that her knowledge in intention extends only as far as the fact that she is *trying* to write those words on the blackboard. I urged that such a picture conflicts with a central thought in Anscombe's treatment of practical knowledge.

The most obvious alternative is a *disjunctive* conception. To have practical knowledge of a happening that is one's doing something intentionally is to know that happening 'from inside', as its agent. One's knowledge in intention embraces the features of what is happening in objective reality that figure in one's intention, even though – this is the other disjunct – one can be wrong in taking oneself to be doing such-and-such because of malfunctioning chalk and the like.

Much work, which I am obviously not going to do now, would be needed for a proper elaboration of this. I shall end by proposing this way of framing the thought: our intentional interventions in the world are themselves cases of our conceptual capacities in operation. Conceptual capacities, in the relevant sense, are capacities that belong to reason, and they include capacities not only for discursive thought but also for acting. An exercise of a practical conceptual capacity is, to put things as I did earlier, a practical assent to acting in a certain way. If the fallibility that belongs to any such capacity does not kick in, assenting to acting in a certain way can itself be intentionally acting in that way, realizing the concept of acting in that way; that is what practical assent is, absent such factors as malfunctioning chalk, if the occasion of the assent is the occasion for the acting assented to.[9] And intentional interventions in the world, like any actualizations of capacities that belong to reason, are as such self-conscious, and hence within the purview of a capacity, fallible because of things

---

[9] The proviso is to leave room for practical reasoning that addresses the question what to do on some future occasion. This should not dislodge the idea that when the question addressed by practical reasoning is what to do now, drawing the conclusion is acting.

like the risk of malfunctioning chalk, for knowledge that is not a reality distinct from what is known, as observational knowledge is.

Anscombe's conception of practical knowledge can be framed in those terms. And one thing that is grand about the conception is its radical departure from the philosophical prejudices that underlie familiar sorts of shrinkage in the scope we attribute to immediate self-knowledge. This brings out a resonance for the thesis I have been urging in this chapter: that the proper form of expression for an intention in action is not a statement of what one should be doing but a statement of what one is doing.[10]

---

[10] I mean these closing remarks to echo some of the wording in Sebastian Rödl's wonderful book *Self-Consciousness* (Cambridge, Mass.: Harvard University Press, 2007); though I think his treatment of practical self-consciousness in ch. 2 is insufficiently responsive to Anscombe's point that reasoning towards the truth of a proposition is not practical reasoning.

5

BEING IN THE WORLD

Joseph Raz

Abstract
Actions for which we are responsible constitute our engagement
with the world as rational agents. What is the relationship between
such actions and our capacities for rational agency? I take this to
be a question about responsibility in a particular use of that
term, which I shall call 'responsibility$_2$'. We are not responsible$_2$ for
all our intentional actions (actions under hypnosis, for example),
but we can nevertheless be responsible$_2$ for actions we do not
adequately control, for negligent actions, and for non-intentional
omissions. Appreciating this helps show that familiar principles of
responsibility are false: those which delimit responsibility to intentional actions or to actions and outcomes under our control. In the
attempt to fashion an alternative principle, cases of negligence
prove pivotal. We hold ourselves and others responsible$_2$ for
conduct within our respective 'domains of secure competence',
(i.e. that within which we are confident of doing what we set
ourselves to do, barring events which defeat our competence),
even when actions within that domain fail. The significance of this
practice of holding ourselves and others responsible$_2$ lies in the way
it maintains our sense of who we are and of how we are related to
the world in which we act.[1]

We actively engage with the world through our actions. Among
them those for which we are responsible hold a special place.
They constitute our engagement with the world as rational agents,
for we are responsible for actions in virtue of their relationship to
our capacities of rational agency. The question of responsibility
is largely the question: what is that relationship, and how does
the criterion for responsibility for action extend to account for
responsibility for whatever else we are responsible for (e.g. for
omissions or for consequences of our actions)?

[1] I am grateful for helpful comments to Penelope Bulloch, Andrei Marmor, Ulrike
Heuer, Rebecca Prebble, Nandi Theunissen, Gideon Yaffe, Barbara Herman, Gary Watson,
David Owens, David Enoch, Jonathan Adler, and to the students in my Fall 2008 seminar,
especially A. Archer, J. Lenowitz, and B. Lewis.

80 JOSEPH RAZ

Following some clarification of the sense of responsibility the chapter is about, Section One briefly criticises two principles of responsibility: one takes us to be responsible only for our intentional actions, and for their intended or foreseen consequences, the other takes us to be responsible only for actions and outcomes which are under our control. I will then take a first step towards an alternative.

1. Responsibility, control and intentions

For our purposes three uses of 'responsible' are of interest[2]:

(1) People are responsible$_1$ if and only if they have the capacity for rational action (as when we say 'he is not in his right mind and therefore not responsible for his actions'). The powers of rational action are more extensive than just our rational capacities (powers of reasoning, of decision etc.) including also perception, memory and control of the body without which one cannot act effectively. While mental actions require relatively limited abilities, when dealing with responsibility for other kinds of actions one has to take account of the abilities which make them possible.

(2) People who are responsible$_1$ are not necessarily responsible$_2$ for everything they do. They may, e.g., act while sleepwalking, or under hypnosis. To be responsible$_2$ their actions must appropriately relate to their capacities of rational agency. Otherwise it is mysterious why only those with capacities of rational agency can be responsible$_1$.

(3) In a different sense having a responsibility$_3$ is like having a duty (as in 'it was your responsibility to secure the building').[3]

My aim is to contribute towards an answer to the question: what relationship between our capacities for rational agency and an

<hr/>

[2] Naturally we are not interested in the use of 'responsibility' to indicate causality (as in 'the earthquake is responsible for the power failure'). Similarly, neither the use of 'is responsible' as a commendation (as in 'you can trust him. He is a responsible fellow'), nor its reverse, namely its use as equivalent to blameworthy (as 'the doctor is responsible for his death' would normally be understood) are of interest.

[3] Responsibility$_1$ is a matter of degree, but at its minimum it is presupposed by responsibility$_2$ and responsibility$_3$. Only those with rational capacities can be subject to duties, and only they can be responsible$_2$.

action makes us responsible$_2$ for the latter? The core question is about a non-mediated relationship between action (say) and the capacity for rational agency that renders one responsible$_2$ for the action. There is widespread agreement on several derivative principles of responsibility$_2$. I will mention only one: *intentional disabling does not disable*: if a person φs, having generated (in ways he is responsible$_2$ for) conditions which would otherwise make him not responsible$_2$ for φing in order to avoid being responsible$_2$ for φing then he is responsible$_2$ for φing. This is barely an extension of direct responsibility$_2$. Since the second act is the intended consequence of the first act one is responsible$_2$ for it to the extent that one is responsible$_2$ for the intended consequences of one's intentional actions. Normally, one is not, at least not without qualification, responsible$_2$ in that way for human actions which one intended to bring about. But one is so responsible$_2$ when one intended the perpetrators of the resulting actions not to be responsible$_2$ for their actions. In such cases any suggestion that the resulting actions break the chain of responsibility$_2$ is removed. For the most part when discussing examples I will assume that derivative responsibility$_2$ does not apply to them, and principles of responsibility$_2$ will be implicitly qualified to allow for the application of derivative responsibility$_2$.

The thought that among our actions we are responsible$_2$ for our intentional actions and only them[4] appears natural to those who think that intentional actions are performed for what their agents take to be reasons for those actions. For then we are responsible$_2$ for actions that are guided by our rational capacities. This inclines some to think that we are responsible$_2$ for actions which are under our control: we control actions by guiding them in light of what we take to be reasons for those actions. The Control Principle, namely that *we are responsible$_2$ for X if and only if X is under our rational control, or only because, and to the extent that X has aspects which are under our rational control*, appears to coincide with the Intention Principle, namely that *we are responsible$_2$ for X if and only if X is an intentional action or a foreseen or intended consequence of such an action*.

This appearance is, however, misleading. Not all intentional actions are under our control. 'Control' is used in a context-sensitive way, and there is no need here to explore the notion, except as it is used in the Control Principle. Roughly it means:

---

[4]   Here I disregard the question of responsibility other than for actions.

82   JOSEPH RAZ

being moved and guided by reasons as one sees them.[5] A simple
example helps in establishing that not all intentional actions are
'under our control'. A drunk who decided to leave the bar,
wobbles his way out, but on his way he bumps into a table, breaking a wine glass. Breaking the glass was unintentional and uncontrolled. But his walking out was intentional, and yet not properly
controlled. Control is a matter of degree. The drunk controlled
his walking sufficiently to get out of the bar, but not well enough
to avoid bumping into the furniture.

Examples suggest that *one controls an action if and only if*

   *(1)   either one performs it because one intends to do so, or one performs
          it, aware that one does so, by performing another action which one
          intends to perform,*
   *(2)   the performance is guided by one's intention and one's beliefs, so
          that to the extent that one's factual beliefs are true one does not, in
          performing the action, do anything else which one believes one
          should not (on balance) do;*
   *(3)   in so far as realisation of the previous conditions depends on
          control of one's body they are securely realised.*

   The thought is that for actions to be controlled it is not enough
that they are motivated and guided by agents' intentions. Control
requires that the guidance reflects agents' views of all the reasons
that apply to the occasion, and ways of pursuing them.[6] And it
requires reliable muscular control. This third condition recognises the distance between cases in which though one is doing what
one intends to do because one intends to do it one is not doing it
intentionally, because the intention does not play its proper
guiding role in directing the action, and cases in which the action
is intentional even though the guidance by the intention is
wobbly. These latter cases are those where the action is intentional
and yet not controlled. But there are other cases of intentionality
without good control, including expressive actions and marginal
intentional actions, like doodling, etc.[7]

---

[5]   See Raz, *Engaging Reason* (OUP, 1999) pp. 11–12.
[6]   If he believes that bumping into the furniture should be avoided, and fails to do so
then his walking is not adequately controlled by him.
[7]   See 'On the Guise of the Good,' and *Engaging Reason*, pp. 36–44. Weak-willed actions
are ones in which our will escapes the control of our rational powers. They require special
consideration they will not here receive.

In common situations the drunk is responsible$_2$ for the walking in spite of lack of control. Some exceptions apart, we are responsible$_2$ for our intentional actions even when we do not adequately control them. Hence, responsibility$_2$ is sometimes independent of control, and does not depend on the relations between action and capacities that control manifests. But neither is the Intention Principle true. We are responsible$_2$ for some non-intentional omissions, and for some of their consequences. Similarly, we are responsible$_2$ for negligent actions, and for negligently produced harm. So the Intention Principle too fails to identify a necessary condition for responsibility$_2$.

Furthermore, we are not responsible$_2$ for all our intentional actions. Actions under hypnosis, e.g., may be intentional, yet the agents are not responsible$_2$ for them. They are not related in the right way to their rational powers, for deliberation about the case for and against them cannot lead the hypnotized to revise their intentions to perform them. This means that neither the Control nor the Intention Principles provide a sufficient condition of responsibility$_2$ either.

2. Engaging with the World

We need a fresh start, and I will take cases of negligence to be pivotal for the understanding of responsibility. Negligence cases are among the paradigm problem cases discussed in writings about moral luck, for responsibility$_2$ for negligence is inconsistent with both Intention and Control Principles.

Williams, who gave the question of moral luck its name,[8] did not focus on responsibility. He identified one attitude people may have to their actions and their consequences which we know by the name he gave it: agent-regret. Commentators observed that he hardly addressed the question he raised, the question of moral luck. True, but he did point to the importance of our attachment to the consequences of our actions, whether or not we control them, manifested in feelings of agent-regret. In doing so he signalled that the way we are attached to our actions and their consequences is key to an understanding of responsibility.

---

[8] Bernard Williams 'Moral Luck' in *Moral Luck* (Cambridge: Cambridge University Press, 1982), pp. 20–39.

Williams pointed out that given the kind of creatures we are we cannot detach ourselves from the unintentional aspects of our actions, a detachment necessary for the elimination of agent-regret. Therefore, such attachments aren't always unjustified. This is not a conclusive argument. To supplement it we need to understand the significance of agent-regret, and related emotions (pride, shame etc.) in our life. If they play a significant role in our life then some instances of them can be justified. Given how fundamental it is to the kind of animals we are no other vindication is needed, and probably no other is possible.[9]

Our sense of who we are is shaped through our actions and experiences. To clarify this commonplace observation we must challenge the identity, often assumed, between matters beyond our exclusive control and matters of luck.

The success of our actions depends on factors beyond our control, but typically they are not matters of luck. People develop skills that enable them to do many things with confidence that they will succeed, barring some extraordinary events like an earthquake or a seizure. Of course, those who accepted Williams's terminology[10] warned that they use 'luck' stipulatively. But the choice of terminology betrays a willingness to imagine our being in the world as being in an alien environment, tossed about on the waves of fortune whenever we venture beyond our thoughts and intentions. An understanding of our engagement with the world should distinguish between the ways we gamble, deliberately taking risks, and the ways our actions, while depending on matters over which we have little influence, are not gambles, and make

---

[9]   A clarification regarding justification: It is sometimes assumed that if an action or attitude is justified then not taking the action or not having the attitude is unjustified. But that is not generally true. Justification, we might say, is permissive. The justification of regret does not imply anything about the justification of its absence. Second, a certain response, say amused laughter, may be justified, say in response to a joke, even though the fact that one is amused by such a joke shows that one has a rather crude taste. The justification of actions and attitudes is, in other words, limited to them, and is consistent with the fact that they may betray unpleasing, or worse, character traits or dispositions. Williams's explanation of the role of agent-regret, even if it succeeds in the cases of *Gauguin* and *Karenina*, does not generalise to justify seemingly justified agent-regret for less dramatically life-transforming decisions. We require an alternative explanation of the significance of our attachment to the consequences of our actions and it will also serve as its vindication: Instances of agent-regret and similar emotions are justified when they are appropriately related to the significance of the emotion.

[10]   Which he introduced tongue in cheek, intending it to be self-undermining, thus leading to the rejection of the 'morality system' (see his 'Postscript' in Statman (ed) *Moral Luck* (State University of New York Press, 1993), p. 251).

plain the roles of these different forms of engagement in the constitution of our sense of ourselves.

The distinction between risk-taking and other actions and activities is inevitably a soft one. But it is important in demarcating two distinct attitudes, with many intermediate ones. At one extreme are gambling[11] and other actions over whose outcome we have hardly any influence, and where we do not have warranted beliefs about their outcome (except, sometimes, about the chances of different outcomes). Here belong along with playing roulette, also more ordinary enterprises, such as hitch-hiking (assuming, perhaps unrealistically, that little skill is involved in hiking).

Other activities are very different. We expect their outcome to depend on our skill and effort. We are aware that they too depend on factors over which we have little influence, but take our skills in using and navigating around such factors to justify confidence that we will succeed. Many activities (cooking, eating, shopping, visiting friends, studying for a degree, etc.) fall into this category. Others are mixed cases. In opening a grocery store I rely on my skill for success, but am aware that an economic downturn, etc., is not unlikely. One is both taking a gamble and relying on resolution and skill to navigate to success.

These two ways in which our activities depend on risk are important in our lives in different ways. The case in which one relies on nature to play along (even though aware that it may not) is crucial to one's ability to act (with a modicum of success) at all. To do so one must learn to assess what is likely or unlikely to happen in the normal course of events, to judge whether one's situation is normal, and to develop skills that assure one of success in the normal case, by testing one's skills to their limits. That is how we learn when we can trust our skills, and depend on nature (including other agents) co-operating, and when we are placing ourselves at the mercy of luck.

Unless I can trust the chair to carry my weight, the ground not to give way when I walk, the plate to maintain rigidity when I hold

---

[11] One gambles when taking the risk is an end in itself or a means for the end of gaining whatever is the prize for winning. In other cases in this category, the risk is not the means to the end, but merely a feature of the situation one puts up with. Gambling does not pose the problem for the Control Principle that other risk-dependent outcomes do. Either one is not responsible for the outcome at all, or in cases one is, one knowingly undertook the risk of that outcome, and in so doing as it were consented to the outcome.

it, etc., I cannot perform even the simplest act. More complex acts require similar understanding of one's environment, though to a higher degree.

Learning how to perform actions mostly involves developing and honing the needed skills by trying to perform them, testing the limits of one's abilities and skills as one expands them. Failure is an essential part of the learning process, a process that for the most part is not separate from normal acting. For the most part, the learning is concurrent with the acting. The pianist improves as he practices, gives recitals, makes recordings, etc. Failure remains, throughout one's life, part of learning, solidifying, and reassuring one about one's skills and their limits.

That is in large part how we make ourselves. Who we are, in the relevant sense, is determined by dispositions and attitudes that incline us to pursue some goals and keep clear of others. And these dispositions are shaped in part by our skills, and our aware-ness of them, by our self-image as people who, aware of their abilities, are willing or unwilling to challenge their limitations, to run or to avoid certain risks, etc.

To summarise: *First*, our life, its successes, failures and meaning, are bound up with our interaction with the world, our impact on it and its impact on us. *Second*, while in some of our activities we put ourselves at the mercy of luck, and sometimes that may be the point, the thrill, of it, in others we rely on our skills, confident, to various degrees, that we know how to succeed given normal con-ditions. *Third*, our sense of who we are while in part determined independently of our activities (say by gender or ethnicity and their social meanings) is in part determined by our sense of our abilities and their limitations (against the background of the natural and social environment of our life), which (in ways depen-dent on our temperament and dispositions) fixes the limits of our ambitions and aspirations. *Fourth*, that sense of who we are is continuously being moulded through our understanding of our actions, which reinforce, extend or undermine our confidence in our abilities and skills.[12] *Fifth*, the process of shaping who we are is normatively driven, that is we form views of who or what we want to be in light of views of what people like us should be. *Sixth*, our actions and their success both reveal who we are and make us who we are, in ways that are often difficult to disentangle.

---

[12] Though some actions affect us not gradually, but dramatically.

The connection between our actions and who we are explains why emotions like agent-regret which express our feelings about who we are, who we are becoming, or have become (or may become), apply to our actions, including aspects of them which exceed our control. Regarding any instance of such a feeling the question of its justification is a question about the appropriateness of taking that view of the significance of the action to who we are.

3. Responsibility$_2$ and the Control Principle

These reflections on the sense of control and of luck help clarify responsibility$_2$. For one thing they suggest that the Control Principle reaches further than is sometimes recognised.

First, we are (normally) responsible$_2$ both for our intentional actions and for intentions to perform actions. But given that responsibility$_2$ for intentional actions is determined not merely by the intentions (if any) to perform them, but by being guided and controlled by our intentions and beliefs throughout at least a significant part of their performance, different degrees or kinds of praise or blame may be appropriate.

Second, we control not only attempts. Often, we control intentional acts, including their results.[13] Skilled in performing the actions, our movements are adjusted to the circumstances securing the intended result, and avoiding others that we believe we ought to avoid. Hence, it is a mistake to hold that necessarily if a person is responsible$_2$ and to blame for an act, then the blame he deserves is the same as the blame he would have deserved had he been responsible$_2$ for an unsuccessful attempt to perform it. For it is not true that agents control only what constitutes an attempt to perform their actions, or what, had they failed, would have constituted such an attempt.

What of cases in which we are subject to luck, as when we bet on the horses, or make speculative investments? It is easy to misperceive the role of intention in such actions. While I intentionally place a bet, I do not intentionally win the bet, rather, luckily I win. I intentionally invest speculatively, and I may even intend to make

---

[13] I am using 'result' in the sense stipulated for it by von Wright, i.e. the end state which the action is defined as bringing about. See von Wright 'On the Logic of Norms and Actions' in *Philosophical Papers* (Blackwell, 1983), p. 107.

my fortune thereby. But I do not intentionally make a fortune
through that investment. It just happens to turn up trumps, as I
hoped that it would.

The divide is anything but sharp. The more skill and foresight
goes into the action the more appropriate it is to say that I
intended its result. For my argument the absence of a sharp
boundary does not matter, for I reject the Control Principle. At
the present stage of the argument all I am claiming is that quite
often when acting intentionally we are in control of the result.
That makes it appropriate for the nature of the result, and not
only the character of the intention or attempt, to affect the appropriate blame or praise.

What could motivate rejecting this conclusion? Perhaps that
the action successfully completed might have failed had factors
beyond our control intervened? But that can only establish that
had we failed because of such factors our failure would have been
beyond our control. It does not establish that as things were we
were not in control of the action and its result.

Another thought is that our successfully performing the action
depended not only on our intention but also on other factors, (we
got from the street to the kitchen because the lock functioned,
the floor supported us, etc.). Because we do not control these
factors the action is not under our exclusive control. But that is a
non-sequitur. The action is under our control in the required
sense because we adjusted it to the factors which are beyond our
control. We took advantage of them, avoided difficulties they
presented, etc. That is the way control is exercised when we act.

Third, we are sometimes responsible$_2$ for beliefs and emotions
and not only for actions. Robert Adams reminds us that people
are often held responsible for their emotions (e.g. for excessive
anger, for jealousy), for their beliefs (e.g. that some races are
inferior to others), and for other attitudes (e.g. self-
righteousness) and are blameworthy or praiseworthy for them.
Adams explains that:

> *To refuse to take responsibility for one's emotions and motives is to be
> inappropriately alienated from one's own emotional and appetitive
> faculties.*[14]

---

[14] R.M. Adams, 'Involuntary Sins' 94 *The Philosophical Review*, 3 (1985), p. 16. I believe
that most of the sins Adams deals with are neither voluntary nor involuntary. They are

Adams recognises that the claim has to be restricted to a subclass
of psychological phenomena:

> . . . *among states of mind that have intentional objects, the ones for*
> *which we are directly responsible are those in which we are responding,*
> *consciously or unconsciously, to data that are rich enough to permit*
> *a fairly adequate ethical appreciation of the state's intentional*
> *object . . .* [15]

The explanation is both correct, and up to a point, consistent with
the Control Principle. We control our beliefs and are in control of
our emotions, desires, intentions and actions in so far as we
respond to reasons as we see them, and have those beliefs, emotions, desires and intentions which we take to accord with reason.[16] In fact Adams rejects the Control Principle altogether.[17] So
do I. The next sections examine my reasons.

psychological phenomena to which the distinction does not happily apply. See for more
detailed discrimination J. Raz, *Engaging Reason* pp. 11–12. Adams identifies the voluntary
with what is chosen or meant (see Adams, *op. cit.*, at p. 3). That seems to me inaccurate. See
my discussion in *Engaging Reason* at pp. 12–14.

[15] Adams, *op. cit.*, at p. 26.

[16] *Engaging Reason* ch. 1, see also David Owens, 'Rationalism About Obligation' 16(3)
European Journal of Philosophy p. 403 (2008), Susan Hurley, *Natural Reasons* (OUP, 1989).

[17] I am not clear what his view is. He writes: 'whereas the traditional theories are
concerned with *conscious* recognition of the badness of the act, my criterion demands only
that the data to which we are responding be rich enough to *permit* recognition of the
relevant values. . . . it would not be plausible to limit our responsibility for states of mind
to cases in which we are or should have been conscious (so as to be able to say) that we
are responding to those data'. (Adams, *op. cit.*, at pp. 26–7) As responsiveness to reason
involves some degree of self-awareness the passage suggests a rejection of the Control
Principle, at least if control is understood as responsiveness to reason. He also rejects a
negligence standard in rejecting that the limit is at what we should have been aware of, and
also in his earlier remarks about Alan Donagan who 'maintains . . . [that] "Ignorance . . . is
culpable if and only if it springs from negligence- from want of due care" . . . Negligence,
in this context, is a voluntary omission of actions that one ought to have performed and
that would have cured or prevented the ignorance.' (at p. 19) But as Adams misinterprets
here the nature of negligence, this is consistent with his view coinciding with setting a
(properly understood) negligence limit to responsibility. Indeed later on he remarks 'I
take it the imaginary Hitler Jugend alumnus . . . has rich enough data in his evidence of the
humanity of the non-combatants in question, even if he is never told that they have rights.
This will normally be true even if he has never met a member of the race or ethnic group
to which the non-combatants belong; it is enough to know that they are human beings. On
the other hand, I am prepared to grant, for example, that some conception of a preferable,
workable alternative system may be part of the data needed for a fairly adequate appre-
ciation of the injustice of a social or economic system, and that one's experience and
education may leave one innocently unable to imagine such an alternative' (at p. 27) which
suggests endorsing a negligence principle.

4. Responsibility₂ and the domain of secure competence

One type of case in which responsibility$_2$ is inconsistent with the Control Principle involves cases in which people are responsible$_2$ for actions which they do not control adequately, and because of that they are also responsible$_2$ for another, accidental action. The person who picks up a vase, which slips from his fingers and breaks, and the driver whose foot 'accidentally' slips off the brake, causing an accident, are examples. There was nothing wrong in the person who broke the vase picking it up, and the driver driving. But they did not control these actions adequately, and the common judgement, and it is correct, is that they are responsible$_2$. But why?

Two principles are involved. If they are responsible$_2$ for handling the vase and for driving even though they do not control these actions then they are responsible$_2$ for breaking the vase and for the accident. This responsibility$_2$ arises because of another principle of derivative responsibility$_2$, whereby one is responsible for some of the consequences of actions for which one is responsible$_2$. I will not stop to define or defend the principle here.[18] The question I wish to explore is why are they responsible$_2$ for actions they do not control in the first place? Because of the special standing of a domain of secure competence. I have argued that central to our way of being in the world is a permanently evolving sense of our own mastery and its limitations. Our sense of ourselves includes awareness of a domain within which we are confident that, barring competence-defeating events (a seizure, a biased teacher, etc.), if we set ourselves to do something we will. I will call it the *domain of secure competence*. The crucial point is that we hold ourselves and others responsible$_2$ for conduct within our respective domains of secure competence, and we do so even when actions within the domain fail, if the failure is not due to a competence-defeating event.

This is an observation about how we judge matters: When the glass we put on the table tumbles off it, when while taking a step towards the door we bump into the table, etc., we tend to feel annoyance, and to blame ourselves. In these and other reactions we show that we take ourselves to be responsible$_2$ for these actions.

---

[18] See 'Responsibility and the Negligence Standard' *Oxford Journal of Legal Studies* 30 (2010) pp. 1–18.

Moreover, these reactions are accepted as appropriate, so long as they are not based on mistakes about our domain of secure competence, do not ignore the occurrence of competence-defeating events, and are not disproportionate. Section 2 provided the root of an explanation: We develop our sense of who we are in part by evolving and becoming aware of our secure competence. That recognition takes a normative form: if an act is of kind within our secure competence we hold ourselves responsible$_2$ for it (e.g., putting down the vase), or for doing whatever we happen to do in failing to perform it (e.g., breaking the vase).

Failure to control conduct within our domain of secure competence threatens to undermine our self-esteem and our sense of who we are, what we are capable of, etc. We must react to it. We may conclude that we are no longer able to securely perform that action. We have grown frail, our competence is diminishing. We come to recognise our limitations. Commonly that is not the case, and we do not allow it to be. We assert our competence by holding ourselves responsible$_2$ for it. To disavow responsibility$_2$ is to be false to who we are.[19]

I am both drawing attention to the practice of holding ourselves responsible$_2$ for actions within our respective spheres of secure competence and justifying it, by pointing to its role in maintaining our sense of who we are, and of our relations to the world. So it misses the point to counter-argue that my observations are guilty of *petitio principii*, that we are false to ourselves if we deny responsibility$_2$ for failed actions within our sphere of secure competence only if I am right, which remains to be established. My argument, such as it is, simply points to our practice of ascribing and acknowledging responsibility$_2$, in a way that enables us to understand its significance in our life. We should, however, expect an additional vindicating explanation of the practice, one that relates it to our capacities of rational agency.

Before giving my explanation, I will discuss two alternatives. The first regards responsibility$_2$ for intentional but uncontrolled action as derivative from responsibility$_2$ for the intention or from the attempt to act on it. It is unsatisfactory partly because such actions need neither be attempted in a controlled way, before we lose control of them, nor performed with an independent

---

[19] Adams's observation quoted earlier though confined to our emotions applies to actions as well: 'to refuse to take responsibility for one's emotions and motives is to be inappropriately alienated from one's own emotional and appetitive faculties.'

intention. They may be expressive actions or other acts whose intentionality is embedded, not arising out of an independent intention. Besides, there is the difficulty of justifying the principle of derivative responsibility$_2$ relied on. An explanation which is a variant of mine (below) for underivative responsibility$_2$ would not explain why the responsibility$_2$ is merely derivative.[20]

The second, more radical, alternative is that we ought to control actions that lie within the domain of secure competence. According to it while other duties, other practical reasons, do not establish responsibility$_2$, duties of control are special and do just that. It is true that duties to control our actions differ radically from other duties. Moreover, in many of the relevant cases we ought to have controlled our actions. But these duties do not explain why we are responsible$_2$ for the actions we should have controlled. They are, or are analogous to, instrumental duties. Since I ought not break the vase. If I control my actions it will not break. Therefore I ought to control my actions. But note that where there is no sound end to which control is a means or a prerequisite, there is no duty to control. But responsibility$_2$ for these actions is not conditional on having a duty to control them. We are responsible$_2$ for them, so long as they belong within our sphere of secure competence. As with other duties, failure to comply with duties to control counts against us only if (on independent grounds) we are responsible$_2$ for the actions that constitute such failure.

The explanation lies elsewhere: the sphere of our secure competence demarcates the basic domain in which we are competent rational agents, capable not only of planning and intending, but of acting. It is the area in which our capacities of rational agency are available to us. And that is the connection we were looking for: we are responsible$_2$ because we are rational agents, but only for those actions (we can extend the conditions to consequences later) regarding which our capacities of rational agency were available to us to guide and control our actions.

Their availability does not mean that we did control the action, or would have controlled it had we tried harder. We are always liable to fail to control actions within our sphere of secure competence, even when no competence-defeating condition ob-

---

[20] Importantly, the relation of an intention to the action it guides is not that of a means to an end.

tained. The conditions establishing that the action is within the sphere of secure competence apply to action-types. It does not follow that in an individual case where we did not control the action we could not. 'Can' and 'could not', having to sustain counterfactuals, must be generic rather than specific to the occasion. When applied to a specific act 'you can do it now', when it does not mean 'you have the opportunity to do it now' (conditions are right for successful performance) means you will succeed if you try. It need not presuppose the 'can' of ability.

Before further examining this principle of responsibility$_2$ consider complications in its application to the area of secure competence. The process by which people develop their sense of their secure competence is complex, and influenced by the fact that among various social subgroups certain views about what everyone should be able to securely do (walk, climb stairs, hold objects, etc.) prevail, and people tend to develop those competences. Beyond that basic domain of common competence various individuals develop further more advanced competences, following their inclinations and capacities.

Some people are disabled, and disability is (by a stipulative definition) the inability to control a range of conduct that is commonly taken to be conduct that should be within people's domain of secure competence. There are well-known disadvantages in being identified publicly as disabled. Therefore, people on the borderline of disability often prefer to avoid seeing themselves and being seen by others as disabled. They do so by holding themselves responsible$_2$ for conduct that they believe they should control (usually because of a common view that everyone should have it within their secure competence), even when their control of it is not fully secure. Needless to say, often others accept them at their word, i.e. as responsible$_2$ for conduct of that kind.

Furthermore, when people fail to do what they should have been competent to do, should have done, and tried to do, the question whether the failure was due to the fact that they were not as competent as they should have been, or whether they did not try hard enough, or whether their action just failed as some do, does not always have an answer. The boundaries between 'one's competence is not up to the required level', 'one did not try hard enough', and 'one just failed', are indeterminate. Often there is no fact of the matter as to which category an individual case belongs to, and where there is it is rarely possible to be sure about it. Hence, absent manifestation of disability, the practice of holding people responsible₂ for actions which, by a reasonable social standard, they are expected to have within their domain of secure confidence, is justified.

This may seem harsh on individuals who cannot help the situation. But that is not so. Responsibility₂ applies only to people who should have had that competence and control, and that means that they could have had it. It does not apply in the same way to young children, etc. I conclude that the practices I have described are, unless pushed to extremes, reasonable given their role in human life.

5. The case of omissions

Sometimes we are responsible₂ for not doing something. In the absence of a better word I will refer to not-φing as omitting to φ. As noticed earlier it seems impossible to explain responsibility₂ for omissions by reference to either Intention or Control Principles. As we are responsible₂ for many unintentional omissions the Intention Principle fails, and the very notion of control of omission is obscure. Suppose an omission is controlled if the agent would not perform the action unintentionally, and that condition is secure. Given this understanding, control is not necessary for responsibility₂. People who due to some medical condition (e.g. Parkinson's disease, Tourette's syndrome) cannot control some of their omissions may well be responsible₂ for some of them. Besides, this version of the Control Principle does not establish any relationship between controlled omissions and the capacities of rational agency (and cannot therefore be sufficient for responsibility₂ either).

As we omit an indefinite number of actions at any given time, and never have occasion to think of almost all of them, it seems plausible to expect that there is no clear demarcation between those omissions we are responsible₂ for and others we are not, except where there is reason to refer to those omissions, for example, because they were wrong, or advisable. The demarcation that I propose below is suggested by general theoretical considerations, and is by and large consistent with other concerns.

Consider unintended omissions. They are unintended because the question whether or not to perform the omitted action was not fully resolved in the agent's mind. To simplify assume that it was not resolved because it did not arise. I will assume that in-between cases (ambivalence etc.) could be explained once responsibility$_2$ for intended omissions and for omissions that never surfaced in the agent's mind is understood. Distinguish two kinds of cases in which at the time it did not occur to the agent to consider whether to perform the action or omit it. One is due to a failure in the rational functioning of the agent (he intended to set the alarm, but it slipped his mind and he did not). In the other kind of case so far as the agent's beliefs, resolutions, intentions or other attitudes are concerned there is nothing to make him even consider whether to perform the action. For example, I did not call the person whose name is first in the Munich telephone directory today.

We are responsible$_2$ for clear cases of the first kind, and not responsible$_2$ for clear cases of the second. Had I functioned properly as a rational agent then given the person I am, that is given my beliefs, intentions and attitudes, I would have set the alarm. My failure to do so was a failure to connect my various beliefs, intentions, etc. My omission is due to failing to function adequately as a rational agent, even though my capacities of rational agency were available to me (I was not drugged, do not suffer from amnesia, etc.). It was an occasional lapse of functioning just like the case in which I drop the vase. Omitting to call that person in Munich was not due to failure to function as a rational agent, because there was no fault in my functioning as a rational agent in not thinking about the question at all, in not noticing it as a possibility.

How far does the 'failure to connect', in ways which render us responsible$_2$ for omissions, go? It certainly extends well beyond the example of accidentally failing to act on a prior intention. In particular it includes cases in which one 'should have known better', that is some cases in which one failed to consider the case for an action because there was nothing in one's beliefs to suggest such a case, provided that a fairly minimal degree of reflectiveness would have made one change one's beliefs and not because of any new information. Had he been reflective he would have easily realised that an additional belief is implied by his existing beliefs, and that belief in combination with his other beliefs and attitudes would have indicated a case for considering that action. This too is a case of failing to connect: a case in which had he connected he would have modified his existing beliefs and attitudes.

Needless to say there are other examples of failing to consider an action due to 'failing to connect'. Obviously, the boundary is anything but determinate. If I am right that indeterminacy is a feature of our concept of responsibility$_2$ then a good account would preserve it. One confession of a possible drawback in the account: it may well lead to classifying some cases often taken as excuses for wrongful omissions due to ignorance as cases in which one was not responsible$_2$ for the wrongful omissions.

6. The emerging conception of responsibility$_2$

I focused on three types of case: (1) responsibility$_2$ for normal (intentional and) controlled action, where the qualification 'normal' excludes responsibility$_2$ for intentional and controlled action under hypnosis or other conditions which suspend one's ability to function as a competent rational agent; (2) responsibility$_2$ for uncontrolled action within one's sphere of secure competence[21]; (3) responsibility$_2$ for omissions due to failure to integrate one's beliefs, intentions, etc. What I said about them is a bare outline of an account, leaving much to be fleshed out. Arguably, however, all cases of responsibility$_2$ can be analysed as combinations of these three and of principles of derivative responsibility$_2$. For example, the drunk wobbling his way out of the bar and accidentally breaking a wine glass is responsible$_2$ for breaking the glass derivatively, because he is responsible$_2$ for walking. And he is responsible$_2$ for walking derivatively because he is responsible$_2$ for setting out to leave the bar unaided. Why then is he responsible$_2$ for the latter? It is tempting to reply that he should not have started walking as he did. He should have stayed at the bar, or asked the bartender to help him. Perhaps so. But doing what one should not does not establish responsibility$_2$ for that action. Central to the notion of responsibility$_2$ is that actions, good bad and indifferent, are neither to one's credit nor discredit unless one is responsible$_2$ for their performance. The drunk is responsible$_2$ for setting out to walk because it was an action within his sphere of secure competence. So is walking, but not when he is drunk. But deciding not to walk is, even when ordinarily drunk. To be sure, there is a degree of inebriation which would suspend his capacity to function as a rational agent altogether. The example is of a case where this is not so.

---

[21] As the examples show responsibility$_2$ for actions within the sphere of secure competence exists only when they are intentionally initiated.

It is no coincidence that all cases of responsibility$_2$ belong to one or more of the three categories I discussed (with or without the aid of derivative principles). The order of presentation above started in the conventional way: with normal intended and controlled actions. The force of examples (negligence, unintended omissions, etc.) made us revise the Intention and the Control Principles. Yet the impression that normal intended and controlled actions form the central case remains. In a way they do: they are the paradigmatic cases of rational agents successfully deploying their powers of rational agency. But there is another way of looking at matters, which shows responsibility$_2$ for unintended omissions and actions within one's secure competence to be the core of responsibility$_2$. They mark the most basic domain in which agents' rational powers are available (agents are not asleep or drugged, etc.) and functioning (as they automatically are when available), even though not always perfectly.[22]

In remarks about what makes people persons, or rational agents, it is common to emphasise the ability to distance oneself from one's beliefs, commitments, and intentions, to review them and revise them. Equally essential, presupposed even by the ability to review and revise, is the ability to act with confidence, without the need to review, double check or reassure oneself. That competence – applying to forming beliefs, intentions, etc., and to actions alike, is essential if we are not to be stuck in loops of indecision. Moreover, we need to be aware (at least to a degree) of that competence. That awareness, which need not reach the level of explicit articulation, constitutes part of our understanding of who we are, and plays a major role in forming our dispositions to engage with or distance ourselves from various possibilities, prospects or risks. Being responsible$_2$ for actions which manifest, successfully or otherwise, that competence is part of the way (in our existing practices) that boundary of the self, and that sense of who we are, are acknowledged.

I discussed these matters when defining the notion of a zone of secure competence. It was defined in relation to secure skills in performing various actions, but it can be extended to apply to competence in reasoning, mental arithmetic, kinds of memory,

---

[22] But the failure is not normative. It does not mean that we behaved in ways that we should not have. It means merely that had our faculties of rational agency functioned properly then, given our existing beliefs, intentions etc. we would have considered whether to act or to omit (whether or not there was reason to do so, or it was best to do so).

resoluteness and other mental phenomena. The same rationale applies to the type of unintentional omissions for which we are responsible$_2$. It applies to those omissions where a moderate degree of successful functioning of our rational capacities would have alerted us to the need to consider the case for certain actions. In other words, it applies to a minimum competence in rational functioning that is essential to being a rational agent. The sense of who we are and the skills and competences which under-lie it continuously evolve during our life. As I explained, part of the case for not excluding these cases of unsuccessful functioning of our capacities for rational action from responsibility$_2$ is that the inevitable occasional lapse in their functioning is not a result of the capacities and skills being degraded, or of their contracting. Similarly, acknowledging others to be the people they take them-selves to be includes accepting their responsibility$_2$ in such cases. I did not claim that we would not be rational agents if we did not have the concept of responsibility$_2$ which we have, merely that we do have that notion, and that it plays a significant role in our understanding of the way we act in the world.

6

MORAL SCEPTICISM AND AGENCY:
KANT AND KORSGAARD

Robert Stern

Abstract
One argument put forward by Christine Korsgaard in favour of her constructivist appeal to the nature of agency, is that it does better than moral realism in answering moral scepticism. However, realists have replied by pressing on her the worry raised by H. A. Prichard, that any attempt to answer the moral sceptic only succeeds in basing moral actions in non-moral ends, and so is self-defeating. I spell out these issues in more detail, and suggest that both sides can learn something by seeing how the sceptical problematic arises in Kant. Doing so, I argue, shows how Korsgaard might raise the issue of scepticism against the realist whilst avoiding the Prichardian response.[1]

This chapter is about moral scepticism, but also about agents and their actions: in particular, can reflection on the nature of agency be used to address moral scepticism? Within the contemporary literature, Christine Korsgaard is well-known for arguing that it can, while her approach is widely taken to be Kantian. At the same time, one prominent criticism of her position has been that is succumbs to difficulties famously highlighted by H. A. Prichard, that all attempts to answer the sceptic who asks why they should act morally end up undermining themselves, as they only succeed in treating moral actions as a means to non-moral ends – where this may also be taken to be a Kantian worry. After showing how Korsgaard makes herself seem vulnerable to this sort of objection by the way in which she presents her sceptical target, I want to then claim that Kant himself sees the sceptical challenge in a way

[1]   I am grateful to those who commented on this chapter at the *Ratio* conference at which it was first delivered, and also those who heard it as Royal Institute of Philosophy lecture at the University of York – where I am particularly grateful for discussions with Christian Piller on that occasion and subsequently. I would also like to thank Max de Gaynesford for his kind invitation to contribute to the *Ratio* conference and to this collection.

Agents and Their Actions, First Edition. Edited by Maximilian de Gaynesford. © 2011 Blackwell Publishing Ltd. Published 2011 by Blackwell Publishing Ltd.

that avoids Prichardian difficulties. I will then close by suggesting that if we read Korsgaard along these Kantian lines, we can understand her appeal to agency in a way that also avoids becoming a self-undermining response to moral scepticism, and thus put her debate with her critics in a different light.

1. Korsgaard on moral scepticism and practical agency

Korsgaard's treatment of moral scepticism may be seen as part of a broader project in metaethics, which is to argue for constructivism and against realism, where her claim here is that the former has the advantage of being able to respond to moral scepticism in a way that the latter cannot. This scepticism comes about, she argues, when we are faced with what she calls 'the normative question', which arises when we encounter a moral demand, and find it to be problematic:

> The normative question is a first-person question that arises for the moral agent who must actually do what morality says. When you want to know what a philosopher's theory of normativity is, you must place yourself in the position of an *agent* on whom morality is making a difficult claim. You then ask the philosopher: must I really do this? Why must I do this? And his answer is his answer to the normative question.[2]

Korsgaard then goes on to complain that realism does not and cannot answer this question. It *does* not answer it, because all it says is that you must act in a certain way because it is the morally right thing to do, but the question precisely concerns what real force that consideration should have for you.[3] And realism *cannot* answer the question, because on the realist account moral norms

---

[2]   Christine M. Korsgaard, *The Sources of Normativity* [hereafter *SN*], with G. A. Cohen, Raymond Geuss, Thomas Nagel, and Bernard Williams, edited by Onora O'Neill (Cambridge: Cambridge University Press, 1996), p. 16.

[3]   Cf. *SN*, p. 38: '. . . [a]ll [the realist] can say is that it is *true* that this is what you ought to do . . . But this answer appears to be off the mark. It addresses someone who has fallen into doubt about whether the action is really required by morality, not someone who has fallen into doubt about whether moral requirements really are normative'.

and values obtain independently of the agent, so the agent can always question their hold on him and wonder why he must act on them.[4]

Korsgaard argues, therefore, that we must turn from realism to a more constructivist form of metaethics, which instead of starting with reasons and then trying to show the agent why he must follow them, we start with agency and its conditions, and argue that moral norms and values can be constructed out of that in some way. Korsgaard claims that by proceeding in this manner, we can give the normative question an adequate answer, insofar as following the demands of morality and acknowledging its values can be shown to be constitutive of agency itself, so that 'the right of these concepts to give laws to us'[5] will have been established.

How might this strategy work? The argument has a transcendental flavour: that is, the sceptic is shown that they cannot intelligibly reject the demand that morality makes, such as that they must act on the principle of universalizability, or must value the humanity of others, or whatever, because following that principle or acknowledging that value is a necessary condition of being an agent at all;[6] from this perspective, then, just raising the normative question successfully resolves it, as a commitment to these norms and values is already presupposed in being the kind of agent who poses it in the first place, just as a commitment to the principle of non-contradiction is necessary to the kind of mind who wonders if they should follow it.[7] This strategy, Korsgaard thinks, will successfully answer the moral sceptic in a way that the realist does not and cannot, where this is used by her as one of the central arguments in favour of her more constructivist approach.[8]

---

[4]   Cf. Christine M. Korsgaard, *The Constitution of Agency* [hereafter *CA*] (Cambridge: Cambridge University Press, 2008), p. 7: 'The rationalist account . . . cannot explain why rational principles necessarily motivate us. So long as bindingness or normativity is conceived of as a fact external to the will, and therefore external to the person, it seems possible to conceive of a person who is indifferent to it. But this throws doubt on whether such principles can be binding after all'. Cf. also 'The Normativity of Instrumental Reason', reprinted in *CA*, pp. 52–3.

[5]   *SN*, p. 9.

[6]   Cf. e.g. *SN*, pp. 228–9: '. . . I need to will universally in order to see my action as something which *I do*'; and p. 232: '. . . it is the claim to universality that *gives* me a will, that makes my will distinguishable from the operations of desires and impulses in me'.

[7]   Cf. *SN*, p. 235 and *CA*, p. 7.

[8]   Although his constructivism differs from Korsgaard's, David Copp also argues that constructivism is better placed than realism to deal with sceptical issues: see 'A Skeptical Challenge to Moral Non-Naturalism and a Defense of Constructivist Naturalism', *Philosophical Studies*, 126 (2005), pp. 269–83.

2. Prichardian objections to Korsgaard

This, I hope, is a reasonably faithful sketch of Korsgaard's general position and its concerns. Turning now to some assessment of it, we must therefore consider whether it succeeds in its objective of answering 'the normative question' and so dealing with the moral sceptic, and of showing that the realist fails to do so in a way that reveals a serious weakness in the realist's position. In making this assessment of Korsgaard's case, one could of course criticize the details of Korsgaard's argument; but I want to focus instead on a broader strategic challenge to her view, which (following H. A. Prichard's celebrated article 'Does Moral Philosophy Rest on a Mistake?', and related works of his)[9] might be called *the Prichardian challenge*.[10]

The challenge can be presented as follows: to take scepticism seriously in the way that Korsgaard does, is to assume that morality needs some extra-moral basis; however, to be moral is precisely to think the moral reasons one has to act are compelling in themselves, without any such basis for them being required by someone who is a genuine moral agent. So, the Prichardian thinks that all we can really do is remind the sceptic what his moral obligations are, and not get tempted into trying to offer further support for them in some way, as then the sceptic may end up acting morally, but will be doing so for the wrong reasons, so that we have ultimately failed in our efforts to deal with his scepticism.[11] Thus, the realist will claim that the higher wisdom here is not to try to answer the sceptic, but to refuse to engage with him for these Prichardian reasons; as a result, it is argued, Korsgaard's strategy of criticizing the

---

[9] See H. A. Prichard, *Moral Writings*, edited by Jim MacAdam (Oxford: Oxford University Press, 2002).

[10] Korsgaard herself discusses Prichard's position in *SN*: cf. pp. 38–9, pp. 42–44, pp. 60–1.

[11] Cf. John McDowell, 'Are Moral Requirements Hypothetical Imperatives?', reprinted in his *Mind, Value, and Reality* (Cambridge, Mass.: Harvard University Press, 1998), pp. 77–94, p. 86: 'The question "Why should I conform to the dictates of morality?" is most naturally understood as asking for an extra-moral motivation that will be gratified by virtuous behaviour. So understood, the question has no answer. What may happen is that someone is brought to see things as a virtuous person does, and so stops feeling the need to ask it'.

realist for failing to answer the 'normative question' is fatally flawed.[12]

That this is indeed a difficulty for Korsgaard's approach may seem confirmed by passages such as the following:

> I believe that the answer [to the normative question] must appeal, in a deep way, to our sense of who we are, to our sense of our identity. As I have been emphasizing, morality can ask hard things of us, sometimes that we should be prepared to sacrifice our lives in its name. This places a demanding condition on a successful answer to the normative question: it must show that sometimes doing the wrong thing is as bad or worse than death. And for most human beings on most occasions, the only thing that could be as bad or worse than death is something that for us amounts to death – not being ourselves any more . . . If moral claims are ever worth dying for, then violating them must be, in a similar way, worse than death. And this means that they must issue in a deep way from our sense of who we are.[13]

In the light of passages such as these, we might interpret Korsgaard as follows: Morality asks us to act against our immediate interests on many occasions, and thus the moral sceptic might well ask why he should be at all motivated to act as morality demands, and thus why he should consider morality as giving him any *reason* to act. In response, it seems, Korsgaard sets out to show that we cannot act immorally without undermining our agency, which the sceptic presumably wants to preserve. In the end, then, the sceptic can be brought to see that she should not 'experience moral obligation as something alien to her innermost self or her heart's desire',[14] so that a reason for the moral action can be given in terms that will convince her to be moral.

It is precisely this appeal to the apparent interest the agent has and must have in acting morally, however, that has alarmed those who follow Prichard in thinking that to link morality to our inter-

[12] Cf. Gerry Cohen's response to Korsgaard, where he argues that once she allows the sceptic to characterize the problem in the way she does, any prospect of answering him is lost: see *SN*, pp. 178–183.
[13] *SN*, pp. 17–18.
[14] *SN*, p. 240.

ests in this way is to distort what is required, which is that the moral agent should act morally simply because he or she sees what is asked of them. So, for example, Nagel has objected that Korsgaard's approach is in danger of 'cheapening the motive' of moral action, and comes close to being an 'egoist answer to egoism',[15] while Larmore is critical of 'Kantians [who] . . . trace our moral concern for another back to what they regard as our supreme interest – namely, the affirmation of our own rational freedom. Recognizing the moral point of view for what it is really means, in contrast, learning to see the reason to do well by others as a reason that speaks for itself'.[16] Similarly, Watkins and Fitzpatrick have raised the following worry from a realist perspective:

> What is wrong with enslaving someone, for example, seems to be something straightforwardly and simply about her, given what she is – the dignity that belongs to her as a rational being. To cash out the wrongness of such an action and its normative force for me in a way that requires a detour through a story about what I have to do in order to exercise my will at all seems like a move in precisely the wrong direction. It does not seem true to ordinary moral experience, which certainly does not represent other people's value and its significance for us as deriving from commitments bound up with the exercise of our own wills under certain generic constraints inherent in the nature of willing.[17]

---

[15] *SN*, p. 206. Korsgaard responds to Nagel's worry in *SN*, pp. 246–51.

[16] Charles Larmore, *The Autonomy of Morality* (Cambridge: Cambridge University Press, 2008), p. 115. Larmore is spirited in his defence of Prichard's approach at several points in the book, and critical of what he sees as Korsgaard's failure to take Prichard's position sufficiently seriously: see e.g. pp. 90–1, p. 113.

[17] Eric Watkins and William Fitzpatrick, 'O'Neill and Korsgaard on the Construction of Normativity', *The Journal of Value Inquiry*, 36 (2002), pp. 349–67, p. 361. Cf. also David Enoch, 'Agency, Shmagency: Why Normativity Won't Come from What is Constitutive of Action', *Philosophical Review*, 115 (2006), pp. 169–98, where I think Enoch intends to strike a Pritchardian note on p. 180, where he remarks that Korsgaard will end up distorting things if she tries to use the fact that adopting certain principles and values is constitutive of agency as a way of getting the sceptic to be moral: 'However strong or weak the reasons that apply to [the sceptic] and require that he be moral, surely they do not become stronger when he realizes that unless he complies with morality his bodily movements will not be adequately described as actions' – where I take it that Enoch's point is that *if* the sceptic came to think they *were* stronger on this basis, he would then see a reason to act morally, but not in a way that would make his action genuinely moral, so that Korsgaard's strategy here is self-defeating.

Thus, from this perspective, in raising the normative question Korsgaard is in fact said to play into the hands of the sceptic, and so to make precisely the mistake Prichard accused moral philosophy in general of making.

3. Kant and moral scepticism: Sections I and II of the 'Groundwork'

I now want to turn to Kant, and consider how far the issues discussed above turn out to apply to him, and if therefore falls into the same Prichardian trap as Korsgaard seems to do. My strategy will be to argue that while Kant was indeed deeply concerned with a certain type of moral scepticism, this differs from the type discussed above, and so does not lead him to make the mistake of trying to deal with a question that is better left set aside. To keep the discussion within reasonable bounds, I will mainly focus on Kant's *Groundwork of the Metaphysics of Morals*. My claim will be that in the first two sections of the *Groundwork*, the issue of scepticism of any sort hardly arises at all, and that while an important sceptical threat is discussed and dealt with in the third section, this is a threat of a distinctively different kind.

In the Preface and first two sections of the *Groundwork*, it is perhaps scarcely surprising that Kant does not take up any serious sceptical challenge. For, in this part of the work, the main task Kant sets himself is to identify 'the supreme principle of morality', where he does so by taking our commonly shared moral conceptions for granted (for example, about the good will, duty, the imperatival nature of morality, and certain moral cases), and attempting to derive the Formula of Universal Law as the supreme moral principle from them by a process of analysis. In these sections, therefore, Kant seems more than happy to accept that we have a good grasp of morality without any need for philosophy, where he does not expect us to find the Formula of Universal Law to be revisionary of that grasp in any way – indeed, if it were, he would allow that it would be an objection to his claim that it constitutes the supreme principle that he is looking for here. Thus, Kant willingly accepts that in arriving at the Formula of Universal law, he is not teaching 'the moral cognition of common reason' anything new, but simply making it 'attentive to its own principles': 'there is, accordingly, no need of science and philosophy to know what one has to do in order to be honest and good, and even wise and virtuous'.[18] Kant therefore seems to take for granted that our moral practices are in good order and in no need of defence or justification, and that philosophy can proceed by simply reflecting on them, to bring out the fundamental moral principle on which they rely. Given this kind of approach, it is scarcely surprising that sceptical challenges have little place.

Now, Kant is sensitive to a worry that might seem to follow: namely, that if our ordinary moral thinking really is in such good order, and if philosophy must base itself on this thinking, what is the point in engaging with the effort of doing philosophy here at all – particularly, as he admits, when our ordinary thinking is quite adept at a pretty high level of reflection on moral matters, while philosophizing might lead it astray, and so make matters worse.[19] Kant thinks he has a response to this worry – but again, it is a response that so far gives no anti-sceptical role to his philosophical project. For, the value Kant places on philosophy here is that by arriving at the supreme principle of morality, philosophy can lead us to be better moral agents by making it harder for us succumb to the 'natural dialectic' whereby we deceive ourselves on moral matters;[20] its value does not lie in making it easier to answer those who see no reason to be moral.

It may seem, however, that Kant gets closer to addressing a genuine scepticism about morality at the start of Section II, where he raises the spectre of 'those who ridicule all morality as the mere phantom of a human imagination overstepping itself through

[18] Immanuel Kant, *Groundwork of the Metaphysics of Morals*, Akademie edition 4:404; translated by Mary J. Gregor in Immanuel Kant, *Practical Philosophy* (Cambridge: Cambridge University Press, 1996), p. 58 [hereafter *GMM*, where the Akademie reference is followed by the reference to the Gregor translation]. For similar remarks, see 4:412, p. 66, where Kant comments that 'common moral appraisal' is 'very worthy of respect'; and *Critique of Practical Reason* [hereafter *CPrR*], translated by Mary J. Gregor in *Practical Philosophy*, 5:8note, p. 153: '[W]ho would even want to introduce a new principle of all morality and, as it were, first invent it? Just as if, before him, the world had been ignorant of what duty is or in thoroughgoing error about it'.
[19] Cf. *GMM* 4:404, p. 59: '. . . philosopher, though he cannot have any other principle than that of common understanding, can easily confuse his judgment by a mass of considerations foreign and irrelevant to the matter and deflect it from the straight course'.
[20] *GMM*, 4:405, p. 59. For further discussion of this aspect of Kant's position, see Dieter Henrich, 'The Concept of Moral Insight into Kant's Doctrine of the Fact of Reason', in Dieter Henrich, *The Unity of Reason: Essays on Kant's Philosophy*, edited by Richard Velkley (Cambridge, Mass.: Harvard University Press, 1994), pp. 55–87, and Paul Guyer, 'The Strategy of Kant's *Groundwork*', in his *Kant on Freedom, Law, and Happiness* (Cambridge: Cambridge University Press, 2000), pp. 207–31.

self-conceit'.[21] The sceptic Kant is considering here makes much of the frailties Kant has already noted, and who claims that we can therefore never be sure that anyone in fact acts for anything other than self-interest; they then try to bring morality into doubt by pointing to this fact. Kant may therefore seem to getting closer here to an engagement with the moral sceptic.

However, although Kant is indeed bringing in a reference to the sceptical position here, I do not believe that he is taking it seriously in its own right, or setting out to show how it can be refuted as such; rather, he is using it as a means to criticize an empirical approach to moral philosophy, which is his main target. For, Kant holds that the evidence of human moral weakness, and the consequent difficulty of finding clear examples of action done from duty and with no regard for the 'dear self'[22] *can only* lead to scepticism about morality *if* one takes the content of morality to be something we must leave to our experience to determine, by generating this from examples of moral behaviour; for then, if we are truly unable to find any such examples, we could not conduct our investigation into morality, and we might regard all moral principles as suspect. But, of course, Kant thinks anyone who is drawn to this conclusion has simply adopted a mistaken view of the nature of our moral principles, which are known a priori rather than being based on examples – and indeed, must be if we are to treat the moral law as valid for all rational agents, and to explain how we could come up with any moral assessment of the examples of moral action in the first place.[23] Far from taking scepticism here as a serious threat, therefore, Kant uses the possibly sceptical consequences of any empirical approach in ethics as a reductio of that position.

It would seem from the first two sections of the *Groundwork*, therefore, that there is no real evidence to suggest that Kant is seriously troubled by the sort of scepticism identified by Korsgaard. Rather than setting out to refute such scepticism, Kant merely takes the contribution of his enterprise thus far to lie in perhaps enabling us to be better moral beings, in offering us a kind of pure philosophical approach to ethics that will help us

---

[21] *GMM*, 4:407, p. 62. Cf. David Copp, *Morality, Normativity, and Society* (Oxford: Oxford University Press, 2001), p. 5, where Copp cites this passage as evidence of Kant's engagement with the moral sceptic.

[22] *GMM* 4:407, p. 62.

[23] *GMM* 4:408–9, pp. 62–3.

guard against sophistry and self-deception in our moral conduct, while its a priori nature can also help us argue that the lack of clear examples of moral behaviour is no threat to thinking about morality – for example, we can still see how friends are required to be sincere with one another, even if we are not certain that anyone has managed to be motivated solely by friendship and not self-interest.[24] Much like Aristotle, therefore, Kant may be read up to this point as working within a pre-existing moral framework, rather than as trying to answer someone challenging it from the outside and asking why they should adopt it,[25] where this is the sort of project that can lead to the kind of problems raised by the Prichardian.

3. Kant and moral scepticism: Section III of the 'Groundwork'

However, it could now be said, we have so far only discussed Sections I and II of the *Groundwork*, which adopt the analytical approach of starting with our common moral cognition, and so may indeed work in this 'internal' fashion; but (the objection runs) Kant's approach is very different in Section III, with very different results. Moreover, it can be argued, this division in the structure of the *Groundwork* between the first two sections and the last corresponds to the two-fold task that Kant has set himself in the Preface, of not only searching for and identifying the supreme principle of morality (which he claims to have achieved through Sections I and II), but also *establishing* it, or making it good.[26] In addition, he speaks here in terms of offering a 'deduction', which as we know from the first *Critique* is something he associates with justificatory issues. And, finally, it can be pointed out that there are several points in Sections I and II where Kant raises what seem like sceptical concerns about morality and its principles, explicitly

[24] Cf. *GMM*, 4:408, p. 62.
[25] Cf. Aristotle, *Nicomachean Ethics* 1095b1–13. John McDowell, in particular, has empha-sized how it is a mistake to see Aristotle as attempting to offer a 'grounding' for ethics: see the papers on Aristotle reprinted in his *Mind, Value, and Reality*.
[26] Cf. *GMM*, 4:392, p. 47: 'The present groundwork is, however, nothing more than the search for [*Aufsuchung*] and establishment [*Festsetzung*] of the *supreme principle of morality*'. Cf. also *CPrR* 5:8, p. 143, where Kant says that the *Critique* 'presupposes, indeed, the *Groundwork of the Metaphysics of Morals*, but only insofar as this constitutes preliminary acquaintance with the principle of duty and provides and justifies a determinate formula of it [*und eine bestimmte Formel derselben angibt und rechtfertigt*]'.

saying that he will postpone such issues until he gets to Section III: so the fact that Kant has not focused on answering the sceptic in the previous parts of the *Groundwork* can hardly be taken as evidence that he did not take the sceptic seriously, or wanted to leave sceptical worries on one side.

Now, this is all indeed true. So, Kant does indeed characterize his approach in Section III as synthetic rather than analytic; he does give the *Groundwork* a two-fold task; he does speak of offering a deduction; and he does hint at deeper sceptical worries in Section I and II that he promises to return to, where for example he speaks of taking it for granted at this stage that there are practical propositions which command categorically, without having proved that there really are any such propositions.[27] My suggestion now will be, however, that Kant takes this turn in Section III *not* because he is seeking to address here the sort of sceptic who sees no reason to be moral, but rather a scepticism that has a very different basis, and which can thus be addressed without leading to the kind of Prichardian concerns raised above.

To see how Kant's engagement with moral scepticism is distinctive in this way, we must appreciate the *transcendental* character of that scepticism, where this involves a different *kind* of puzzlement about morality than any so far discussed.[28] Whereas the earlier moral sceptic may be characterized as standing 'outside' morality and as asking why they should enter into it at all, Kant's sceptic is more like someone who is already inside the moral life but who nonetheless comes to find it problematic *from within*, and so questions it as a result – where they are not looking for reasons to be moral, but ways of understanding how morality is even possible. What gives rise to this transcendental doubt, Kant thinks, is the way in which morality relates to us *as human beings*, where for us it takes the form of duties that are *obligatory* or *binding* in a particular way, where it is this obligatoriness that raises worries that can lead to deep sceptical concerns about the very possibility of morality.

27   See *GMM* 4:431, p. 82, and 4:425, p. 76.
28   It can be hard to see what is distinctive about such puzzlement. For general accounts to make this clear that I have found helpful, see James Conant, 'Varieties of Skepticism', in Denis McManus (ed.), *Wittgenstein and Scepticism* (London: Routledge, 2004), pp. 97–136; and Robert Nozick, *Philosophical Explorations* (Oxford: Oxford University Press, 1981), pp. 8–11.

Thus, the issue here is whether morality can be made sense of by those already living the moral life, not whether those outside that life can be persuaded into it.

One of the crucial features of Kant's discussion of morality is the contrast he draws between us as moral beings, and the moral life of those with 'holy wills'.[29] The difference, Kant argues, is that whereas for us, morality takes the form of imperatives which tell us what we *must* do, for holy wills this is not the case: for such wills, Kant claims, there is no imperatival force to morality. And because it is an essential feature of morality for us that it involves obligatoriness, Kant thinks that problematic issues are raised here that do not arise for holy wills.

The first, and perhaps most obvious, concerns freedom. For, taking the principle of 'ought implies can',[30] and allowing that morality is obligatory for us, then for morality to be anything more than a 'chimera',[31] we must have freedom. This means, therefore, that a metaphysical basis for moral scepticism can come from a position that denies that we have any such freedom. Indeed, Kant faced a concrete example of such scepticism in the figure of Johann Henrich Schulz, whose work *Attempt at an Introduction to the Doctrine of Morals* was reviewed by Kant in 1783, a couple of years prior to the publication of the *Groundwork*. In his book, Schulz had denied the existence of free will, and thus (as far as Kant was concerned, at least) adopted a 'general fatalism which . . . turns all human conduct into a mere puppet show and thereby does away altogether with the concept of obligation',[32] and thus with all morality. Here, then, is one form of scepticism about morality that has a metaphysical basis, as a threat to the very possibility of morality.

A second metaphysical issue that arises out of the obligatory nature of morality for us as humans, concerns a puzzlement about that obligatoriness *as such*, rather than any doubts one might feel about the freedom that it requires as a condition. What makes that obligatoriness problematic, Kant thinks, is the peculiar kind of *necessity* that the obligations of morality claim for themselves,

---

[29]   See, for example, *GMM*, 4:439, p. 88.

[30]   For further discussion of Kant's attitude to this principle, see my paper 'Does "Ought" Imply "Can"? And Did Kant Think It Does?', *Utilitas*, 16 (2004), pp. 42–61.

[31]   Cf. *GMM*, 4:445, p. 93.

[32]   Immanuel Kant, 'Review of Schulz's *Attempt at an Introduction to a Doctrine of Morals for all Human Beings Regardless of Different Religions*', translated by Mary Gregor in Immanuel Kant, *Practical Philosophy* (Cambridge: Cambridge University Press, 1996), 8:13, p. 9.

where this is problematic not because of issues to do with our motivation or clashes with other concerns, but because it is hard to see what makes a necessity of this kind possible. Just as in the theoretical case, where the problematic nature of the necessity claimed by metaphysicians for their principles can be shown through bringing out the synthetic a priori nature of such claims, where in turn that synthetic a priority is profoundly puzzling, so Kant thinks that the problematic nature of the necessity claimed by morality can be show through bringing out the synthetic a priori nature of what it says we *must* do, in the form of categorical imperatives. It is this issue, therefore, that Kant flags in Section II when he first introduces these imperatives as characteristic of morality, but where he postpones any resolution of it to Section III,[33] in such a way as to put to rest any scepticism about morality based around it, from those who think that perhaps there just *are* no such imperatives of this problematic and mysterious kind, so that Kant is misguided in Section II in deriving any supreme principle of morality from reflection upon them.

In Section II, therefore, Kant sets up the transcendental or 'how possible?' question in the practical case, by contrasting moral imperatives which are categorical, and imperatives of skill or prudence, which are hypothetical. Both types involve a necessity for both tell us that there is something we *must* do; but in the former case, Kant thinks that the necessity is problematic in a way that in the latter case it is not. This is not because the hypothetical imperatives asks us to do something that is in line with our interests, and the categorical imperatives do not, so it is puzzling how we can be motivated to follow the categorical imperatives of morality, or what could (therefore) make such imperatives rational.[34] The difficulty Kant is interested in, I think, is deeper than this: namely, how can it be that there is anything I *must* do, how is such prescriptivity or obligatoriness possible? As Kant puts it: 'This question does not inquire how the performance of the action that the imperative commands can be thought, but only how *the neces-*

---

[33] Cf. *GMM*, 4:419–20, p. 72.

[34] This is perhaps the standard view, expressed for example by Hill when he writes: '. . . Kant held the Hypothetical Imperative to be easier to follow and to justify than the Categorical Imperative. The Categorical Imperative often demands the sacrifice of self-interest whereas the Hypothetical Imperative, typically, is in the service of long-term interest. The Hypothetical Imperative rarely calls for the sort of internal struggle that the Categorical Imperative demands' (Thomas E. Hill, *Dignity and Practical Reason in Kant's Moral Theory* (Ithaca: Cornell University Press, 1992), p. 32).

sitation of the will, which the imperative expresses in the problem, can be thought [or conceived, or made sense of: *gedacht*]'.[35] Kant thinks this question can be answered easily enough in the case of hypothetical imperatives, because there is an analytic relation of containment[36] here: if I want to be a pianist, I must practice, because I cannot be a pianist otherwise, so I am necessarily constrained in this way, by the end I have set myself; and while Kant thinks things are a bit more complicated when it comes to imperatives of prudence, this is not because the connection is any less analytic in theory, but just because it is harder in practice to know about what the necessary means to happiness actually are.[37] In these cases, therefore, it is easy to see how certain actions can come to be represented as necessary for me to do. The problem, however, in the case of the necessity involved in morality, is that this necessity cannot be accounted for analytically as part of the means/end relation, because this relation makes the 'must' conditional on having something as an end, whereas the moral 'must' is unconditional and inescapable and so stronger than this;[38] but then, we lose the way of accounting for the 'must' straightforwardly in analytic terms, as there is now no end in which it can be contained as the required means. If the 'must' in 'you must not tell lies' is not to be explained analytically, therefore, we are left with the question in the moral case of explaining it some other way, which seems much more challenging, and can leave us wondering how there can be any such necessity – just as in the case of metaphysical necessity, we can be left wondering how it can be the case that every event *must* have a cause.

On this approach, therefore, there is a rather precise parallel between how Kant sees scepticism arising in the practical case, and in the theoretical one, where both hinge on the question of how necessity of a certain kind is possible. Thus, as is well known, Kant holds that Hume became a sceptic about causality because

---

[35] *GMM*, 4:417, pp. 69–70, my emphasis.
[36] Cf. GMM, 4:417, p. 70, my emphasis: '. . . the imperative *extracts* the concept of actions necessary to this end merely from the concept of a volition of this end'.
[37] Cf. *GMM*, 4:417–9, pp. 69–71.
[38] Cf. GMM, 4:420, p. 72: '[T]he categorical imperative alone has the tenor of a practical **law**; all the others can indeed be called *principles* of the will but not laws, since what it is necessary to do merely for achieving a discretionary purpose can be regarded as in itself contingent and we can always be released from the precept if we give up the purpose; on the contrary, the unconditional command leaves the will no discretion with respect to the opposite, so that it alone brings with it that necessity which we require of a law'.

he saw on the one had that the necessary relation between events and their causes cannot be accounted for analytically and thus thought of as akin to *logical* necessity, but on the other hand did not see how necessity could obtain otherwise, as anything other than a logical relation. Hume's scepticism is this 'consequent' rather than 'antecedent',[39] based on an apparently well-founded puzzlement concerning the necessity at issue. Likewise, I would argue, Kant saw moral scepticism arising in a similar manner, based on an inability to see how there could even be such a thing as a moral 'must', once the peculiar nature of that 'must' is made clear. And, we cannot console ourselves with the thought that we don't really need to *answer* that question in order to keep morality safe, by thinking that even if we don't know how it is possible, we know at least that in fact agents *are* so bound, because we can see in experience that people's behaviour is governed in this way by nothing but a sense of duty: for, Kant thinks, when it comes to it, this is never really clear, given the murky nature of what really motivates people.[40] Thus, while as a result of Sections I and II of the *Groundwork*, we might agree with Kant about what the supreme principle of morality is, the question still remains how the obligatory force we seem to feel in association with this principle is to be understood and explained, given that no analytic means/end account is open to us; and the worry is, that if no adequate explanation is forthcoming, we will be led to give up the notion of duty as a bad job (much as Hume came to have his sceptical doubts concerning causality), thereby bringing down the whole deontological conception of morality Kant has developed in Sections I and II, and which he thinks is the conception we all share, so that in the end, we would lose our grip on morality altogether. Thus, just as Kant raises the 'how possible?' question in relation to the problem of synthetic a priori knowledge in his theoretical philosophy, so too he raises it in relation to the problem of synthetic a priori practical propositions in his practical philosophy, where those propositions are made synthetic because they express categorical rather than hypothetical imperatives.

[39] Cf. David Hume *Enquiries Concerning Human Understanding and Concerning the Principles of Morals*, 3rd edition, edited by L. A. Selby-Bigge, revised by P. H. Nidditch (Oxford: Oxford University Press, 1975), *An Enquiry Concerning Human Understanding*, Section XII, Parts I and II, pp. 149–60.
[40] Cf. Kant, *GMM*, 4:419, pp. 71–2.

Finally, Kant's conception of the obligatoriness raises a transcendental question concern our moral psychology. For, even assuming that we are free, there is a question about how our psychological structure could work in the way that seems to be required by morality, as Kant conceives it. The difficulty is in seeing how it can be that on the one hand moral action consists in following duty and not inclination, while on the other hand desire and inclination seem to be fundamental to our behaviour as agents – so the question is, how is moral action so much as possible for us? The sceptic Kant is envisaging here is looking for an explanation of how moral agency is possible at all, not a reason to be a moral agent. As Kant says, 'I am willing to admit that no interest *impels* me to [follow the principle of universalisability], for that would not give a categorical imperative; but I must still necessarily *take* an interest in it' if we are to understand how I come to act at all, where what we therefore need is 'insight into how this comes about'.[41]

We have seen, therefore, that for Kant there are three important and interrelated ways in which a kind of transcendental puzzlement about morality can arise, in such a way that if left unchecked, could lead one to feel that morality is a 'chimera' for us, however unproblematic it may be for 'holy wills' who are clearly free, under no peculiar moral 'oughts', and possessed of a different moral psychology.[42] And, I would claim, it is Kant's engagement with these bases for moral scepticism which form the substance of Section III of the *Groundwork*, as we can now briefly set out. In all cases, as we shall see, Kant thinks it is vital to make appeal to aspects of his transcendental idealism, as the only way to settle the puzzlement about morality as it arises in these areas.

As is well known, Kant's response to the worry about freedom is to use his transcendental idealism to distinguish between appearances and things-in-themselves, and thus between a causally

---

[41]   Kant, *GMM*, 4:449, p. 96.

[42]   Jens Timmermann has also emphasized how it is the issue of *explanation* that is at the centre of Kant's engagement with scepticism, rather than the challenge raised by the sceptic who is looking for reasons to be moral. Cf. Jens Timmermann, *Kant's 'Groundwork of the Metaphysics of Morals': A Commentary* (Cambridge: Cambridge University Press, 2007), pp. 129–30, where Timmermann characterizes the question Kant is addressing as one raised by 'that of a morally decent person whose trust in the supreme authority of ethical commands is challenged by the elusiveness of their source as well as the obvious threat of natural determinism', rather than that raised by 'a radical moral sceptic who, say in the face of robust self-regarding interest, asks for a *normative* reason why he should take up the moral point of view at all'.

ordered realm of nature and a non-causal realm, in which the freedom of the moral subject can be preserved. This allows Kant to show how the freedom required to make sense of morality might be possible, while arguing that the fact we feel under moral obligations gives us a practical ground on which to think it is actual, though this can never be established as certain in a theoretical manner as all such knowledge concerning things-in-themselves is denied us.[43]

Kant can also use the dualistic picture of the subject that comes with transcendental idealism to help him explain the peculiar obligatoriness of morality, and so resolve the question of how categorical imperatives are possible. As we have already mentioned, this question only arises from a human perspective, as it is a feature of how morality presents itself to *us*, not to holy wills. Kant then uses this very fact to provide himself with a solution to the puzzle: for, just as it is *because* we have desires and inclinations that morality involves imperatives for us, so he argues that this division within the self *explains* that very obligatoriness, in so far as it is a kind of projection of the fact that the subject's desires set themselves *against* the moral course of action, and so make the latter seem to us to be something to which we are obliged, in a way that does not and cannot happen for the holy will. At the same time, transcendental idealism gives us a framework for this dualistic picture of the self, and how it operates, in such as away as to make the moral 'ought' explicable:

And so categorical imperatives are possible by this: that the idea of freedom makes me a member of an intelligible world and consequently, if I were only this, all my actions *would* always be in conformity with the autonomy of the will; but since at the same time I intuit myself as a member of the world of sense,

---

[43]   Cf. Kant, *GMM*, 4:450–3, pp. 98–100. Although I cannot go into the details here, this is one place where Kant's strategy changes somewhat between the *Groundwork* and the *Critique of Practical Reason*, where I would argue that in the former Kant uses an appeal to transcendental idealism to argue for the division between appearances and things-in-themselves on which his argument for freedom there is presented as depending, whereas in the latter Kant thinks he can place enough weight on an appeal to our moral commitments, and can argue from there to our freedom – a strategy that Kant worried in the *Groundwork* might be question begging (cf. *GMM*, 4:450, pp. 97–8), but which in the second *Critique* he thinks is adequate for what is required (where for our purposes, it is again notable that it would clearly *not* be adequate against a sceptic who just did not recognize any moral commitments as valid in the first place).

they *ought* to be in conformity with it; and this *categorical* ought represents a synthetic proposition a priori, since to my will affected by sensible desires there is added the idea of the same will but belonging to the world of the understanding – a will pure and practical of itself, which contains the supreme condition, in accordance with reason, of the former will.[44]

This, then, is Kant's distinctive answer to the question of obligatoriness that has shaped the debate in the history of ethics between natural law theorists and voluntarists. Kant can be seen as steering a path between both traditions: like the natural law theorists, he treats the rightness of morality in a realist manner, but like the voluntarists he treats the *obligatoriness* of what is right as arising out of the nature of our will with its dualistic structure; and on the other hand, the will that makes morality obligatory is ours and not an external source of reward or punishment like God, while what is thereby made obligatory is fixed by what is right, so that this voluntarism is constrained and does not go all the way down to the content of the moral law itself. In a slogan, therefore, we might say that Kant combined anti-realism about obligatoriness, with realism about that which is obligatory and thus with realism about the right.[45] Once again, therefore, Kant can claim to have offered an answer to someone who questions morality because they just do not see how it can get to have its peculiarly imperatival nature.

Finally, we can also see how Kant uses the framework he has established in Section III of the *Groundwork* to resolve the third source of moral scepticism, which questions the intelligibility of the kind of psychological account that seems required for moral action to be possible. Here, Kant's strategy is to admit that there is indeed something fundamentally puzzling about this, but in a way that we should not feel pushes into anything like moral scepticism: for the puzzlement is in an area where we have good reason to acknowledge that we can only have a limited understanding of such matters, so the fact that we find the issue hard to grasp should not be taken as any reason to doubt the possibility of the phenomenon in question. The difficulty arises, Kant thinks,

[44]   Kant, *GMM*, 4:454, pp. 100–101.
[45]   For further discussion of these issues, see my paper 'Kant, Moral Obligation, and the Holy Will', in Sorin Baiasu and Mark Timmons (eds), *Kant's Practical Philosophy* (Oxford: Oxford University Press, 2011).

because on the one hand morality requires that we act out of duty
and not inclination, while on the other hand as human agents we
are caused to act through our feelings, so that the thought of
something as a duty or what is right for us to do must bring about
such feelings of pleasure in us; but we then become puzzled about
this, because the causal relation here is highly problematic and
mysterious-seeming, because what brings about the feeling of
pleasure is not anything empirical, so we assume that it could only
come about if our action is directed at our happiness, but where
this would render true moral action impossible on the account we
have given of what this must involve. But, Kant argues, rather than
becoming dubious about the possibility of moral action on this
score, we should recognize that the problem just reflects out
general lack of understanding of the relation between the phe-
nomenal and noumenal realms, so that while no positive solution
to the puzzle can be given, there is no reason to jump to a purely
hedonistic model of human action, as here we have a 'blind spot'
that leaves room for the account we need in order to allow for the
possibility of the kind of picture of action as involving duty and
not inclination that is implied by morality.[46]

However, though Kant uses one aspect of his transcendental
idealism here to try to convince us that we must simply accept that
the mechanisms of moral action will always remain mysterious to
us in this way, he also uses another aspect of that idealism to
explain why it is we feel such admiration for our capacity for moral
agency, which again otherwise might seem mysterious in a way
that could lead us to question the value we place upon that
agency. The worry, then, is this:

> [I]f someone asked us why the universal validity of our maxims
> as a law must be the limiting conditions of our actions, and on
> what we base the worth we assign to this way of acting – a worth
> so great that there can be no higher interest anywhere – and
> asked us how it happens that a human being believes that only
> through this does he feel his personal worth, in comparison

---

[46] Cf. Kant, *GMM*, 4:460, p. 106. Kant continues in a similar vein in the following
paragraphs, concluding that given the limitations of our intellects, 'we do not indeed
comprehend the practical unconditional necessity of the moral imperative, but we nevertheless comprehend its *incomprehensibility*; and this is all that can fairly be required of
a philosophy that strives in its principles to the very boundary of human reason' (4:462,
p. 108).

with which that of an agreeable or disagreeable condition is to be held as nothing, we could give him no satisfactory answer.[47]

Here, it may seem, Kant comes closer than at any point so far in trying to answer the non-transcendental sceptic, who asks why they should ignore what is 'agreeable or disagreeable' to them in favour of acting morally, and thus questions the 'validity and practical necessity of subjecting oneself' to the moral principle.[48] However, even here, I would argue, the dialectic is importantly different, as Kant is considering someone who already *does* value their status as a moral being above what is 'agreeable and disagreeable' to them in this way, and who is just wondering 'how it happens' that this is the case – how can the value of being a moral agent be accounted for if *not* in the way in which it furthers my interest?

Now, Kant also uses his transcendental idealism and its dualistic conception of the self to provide an answer to this question, by arguing that the moral self is the *authentic* self, by virtue of its status as a member of the 'intelligible world'; it must thus be given higher value in our eyes, in a way that enables our respect for ourselves and others to be explained, as well as the 'contempt' and 'abhorrence' we feel for ourselves when we fall short.[49] As Kant famously argues, even the most 'hardened scoundrel' is sensitive to this distinction, and therefore wishes that he could be moral even if he can't quite manage it.[50] Kant thus offers an explanation for the admiration we feel for moral agency, and why we value it so highly, thus dispelling the apparent mystery here; but this is a value that will only be apparent to the agent who (even if a hardened scoundrel) has some sensitivity to the moral life, not to the agent who is asking to be brought into that life from the perspective of the egoist or amoralist.

It is not my purpose here to defend in detail the various answers Kant gives to the transcendental sceptic, who raises these 'how possible?' questions against morality, and to ask in particular whether Kant's appeal to the framework of his transcendental idealism actually settles these questions in the way he would like; all I have tried to argue for is the distinctive nature of such

---

[47] Kant, *GMM*, 4:449–50, p. 97.
[48] Kant, *GMM*, 4:449, p. 97.
[49] Cf. Kant, *GMM*, 4:426, p. 77.
[50] See Kant, *GMM*, 4:454–5, p. 101.

questions within Kant's philosophy. And as a result, I would also argue, Kant's position is free of the dangers highlighted by Prichard and others, where it was claimed that the attempt to supply the sceptic with reasons to act ethically has the cost of seeming to distort the very moral phenomena that we are seeking to defend, and so of feeding the sceptical flames; for, nothing in the kind of scepticism that Kant takes seriously is likely to result in his response to that scepticism becoming self-defeating in this manner.

4. Kant and Korsgaard

We began this chapter by considering Korsgaard's constructivist criticism of realism, that it could not offer an adequate response to moral scepticism; and we also began by considering the realist's Prichardian reply, namely that no such response is needed, as to offer one is to seek to give morality a non-moral grounding, in a way that immediately leads us astray. We also saw how Korsgaard might be read as falling into this Prichardian trap.

Following our discussion of Kant, however it should be clear that this dialectic is too simple: for the example of Kant shows how sceptical problems can arise in a way that do not succumb to Prichardian concerns, as these arise from *within* morality. When it comes to Korsgaard, therefore, this opens up a way of reading her 'normative question' in a *transcendental* manner – that is, concerning doubts about morality raised by the need to understand how the moral demand is *possible*, how it can be adequately *explained*, where it is in offering a response to this question that the appeal to the conditions of agency may be said to lie. Understood in this way, Korsgaard could claim to be addressing a form of moral scepticism on the one hand, while avoiding the Prichardian challenge on the other, much as (we have argued) Kant himself manages to do.

Now, there is no space to explore this possibility as an interpretation of Korsgaard in any detail here; the aim has simply been to open it up as a model, by drawing the comparison with Kant. Moreover, it also remains to be seen whether, even understood in this manner, Korsgaard is right to think that constructivism is in a better position to resolve the 'normative question' than the realist: for, of course, the constructivist's transcendental puzzlement has to be properly motivated, and it may be that the realist can claim that some of the puzzlement here is not, but can easily be set aside as spurious. This, again, cannot be considered fully here. It is to be hoped, however, that by considering the interpretation we have offered of Kant, we have also shed light on a strategy Korsgaard can also adopt in answering her Prichardian critics concerning the 'normative question' and thus how her appeal to agency might come to answer it – that is, by treating it as a *transcendental* question, of the sort that might lead to moral scepticism even in the best of us, if it cannot be resolved.

7

SPEECH, ACTION AND UPTAKE

Maximilian de Gaynesford

Abstract
According to J. L. Austin, the performance of illocutionary acts
depends on the speaker achieving the 'uptake' of the audience.
This 'uptake' claim has been employed both in the extension of
speech act theory and in political philosophy, where it forms a
crucial premise in 'silencing' arguments (to regulate the production and distribution of pornography, for example). This chapter
examines Austin's presentation of the 'uptake' claim, asks what he
might have meant by it, clarifies the elements from which a set of
possible interpretations may be derived, and illustrates the main
thrust by noting what has been made of it (I). It then argues that a
basic misapprehension undercuts the possibility of fruitful debate
and offers a modified version of the 'uptake' claim (II). This
modified version calls for explanation, which the chapter makes a
start at providing (III).

Close observation of 'infelicities' prompts the most enlivening
ingenuities in J. L. Austin's *How To Do Things With Words*. Atten-
tiveness to 'the things that can be and go wrong' also guides the
course of the book itself, with its studied deployment of false starts
and backtracking devices.[1] Reflection on action turns to reflection
on failure, which becomes matter for self-reflection, which in turn
guides renewed reflection on action.

If this is the guiding thought of the book, we can put it to use.
Austin claims that 'the performance of an illocutionary act
involves the securing of *uptake*'.[2] He derives this claim precisely
from his investigations of infelicity: that one reason why illocutionary acts sometimes go wrong, why attempts to commit them
fail, is that 'uptake' is not 'secured'. But this 'uptake' claim itself
is not felicitous, and for several reasons. Partly because it is
unclear quite what the claim comes to. Partly because, on the most

---

[1]   *How To Do Things With Words* 2nd edition (Oxford: Oxford University Press, 1975)
p. 114.
[2]   *How To Do Things With Words* p. 117.

Agents and Their Actions, First Edition. Edited by Maximilian de Gaynesford. © 2011 Blackwell
Publishing Ltd. Published 2011 by Blackwell Publishing Ltd.

convincing interpretation, the claim is unsupported and false. But mainly because these aspects of language-use turn out to be a good deal more complex than Austin himself seemed prepared to appreciate, turning as he did almost immediately to other matters.

I

Austin devotes little space to the 'uptake' claim, restricting statement, exposition and argument to a single condensed passage (letters identify the component sentences):

> (a) Unless a certain effect is achieved, the illocutionary act will not have been happily, successfully performed. (b) This is not to say that the illocutionary act is the achieving of a certain effect. (c) I cannot be said to have warned an audience unless it hears what I say and takes what I say in a certain sense. (d) An effect must be achieved on the audience if the illocutionary act is to be carried out. (e) How should we best put it here? And how can we limit it? (f) Generally the effect amounts to bringing about the understanding of the meaning and of the force of the locution. (g) So the performance of an illocutionary act involves the securing of *uptake*.[3]

We might reconstruct the various phases of the passage as follows. Sentences (a) and (d) establish parameters for the 'uptake' claim: concerning illocutionary acts, there is a particular condition on their (happy, successful) performance; this condition has to do with the 'effect' achieved on the audience. Sentences (f) and (g) use these parameters to state the claim itself: the 'effect' required for (happy, successful) performance of illocutionary acts is (generally) a matter of the audience's 'uptake', which is itself a matter of their understanding the meaning and force of the locution. Sentences (b) and (e) clarify and delimit the claim: the achieving of this effect is not to be identified with the (happy, successful) performing of the illocutionary act; the former is merely necessary for the latter. Finally, sentence (c) provides the argument: the 'uptake' claim must hold if we are to make sense of the illocutionary act of warning.

---

[3]   *How To Do Things With Words* pp. 116–7.

Questions arise at each stage. Concerning the parameters, the phrase 'happily, successfully' is (knowingly? intentionally?) infelicitous. The two words pull in two different directions, a divergence that interested Austin and for which he had already provided labels.[4] Suppose there is no 'effect' achieved on the audience. That may mean that the speaker fails outright to perform the illocutionary act he is attempting. 'Successfully' suggests as much. It is then a 'misfire', in Austin's terminology.[5] Or it may mean that there is still something wrong, even though the speaker succeeds in performing the illocutionary act he attempts. 'Happily' suggests this. In the absence of the 'effect', there is something 'not consummated', or 'not implemented', about what is said and done. It is then an 'abuse', in Austin's terminology.[6] Whether what is at stake is a 'misfire' or an 'abuse' makes a considerable difference to the strength of the 'uptake' claim, of course.

The word 'audience' leaves in doubt the class of persons on whom the effect must be achieved. Suppose the effect is not achieved on the audience for whom the speaker intended his utterance. Does that mean that no such illocutionary act is performed? Or would it be sufficient if the effect were achieved on someone who merely happened to hear it?

Questions arise about the statement of the claim. When Austin says 'generally', does he mean that illocutionary acts only 'generally' depend on achieving an effect on the audience, or that it is only 'generally' that this effect, on which *all* such acts depend, takes the form of 'uptake' (i.e. understanding the meaning and force of the locution)? Austin's phrasing surely implies the latter. But this raises further questions. What are the non-general occasions on which achieving the necessary effect is *not* a matter of securing 'uptake' in this sense? And what *is* the effect required on such occasions?

By the 'force' of a locution, Austin means its illocutionary character; for example, that it is meant to warn, to command, to oppose, to praise, to affirm, etc. When Biblical scholars argue over whether *maranatha* is to be interpreted as a petition (Come, Lord), a statement (The Lord has come) or a strong attestation (As surely as the Lord has come, so . . .), for example, Austin

---

4   *How To Do Things With Words* Chapter Two.
5   *How To Do Things With Words* Chapter Three.
6   *How To Do Things With Words* Chapter Four.

would say they are arguing about the force of the expression. But this raises two basic questions about what it is that the audience must 'understand' when they understand the 'force' of a locution. A feature of type-sentences or of their use on a particular occasion? A distinct feature for every distinct speech act verb, or a feature that is common to all verbs of a particular type (e.g. the assertoric and the imperative)?[7]

Delimitation of the claim (or rather failure to do this) also raises questions. Austin leaves it unclear whether it is always and only the speaker's job to secure 'uptake'. Is the illocutionary act performed even if the speaker knowingly and intentionally uses assistance (e.g. assistants) to achieve the required effect on the audience? We might assume Austin would answer in the affirmative. But that leaves cases in which the effect is achieved, but only by means that the speaker does not knowingly or intentionally employ.

Finally, questions arise concerning argument for the claim. Austin appeals to the particular case of warning. He might have tried appealing to a general principle instead: for example, that there is some essential feature F, in virtue of which all illocutionary acts count as such, and F implies the 'uptake' claim. Are we to assume from the fact that he did not attempt an argument in this style that he thought such a principle lacking? Or unnecessary? Or unconvincing? Whatever the truth of this, Austin leaves us without clear indication of how to proceed. Inclusion of verbs like 'warn' in locutions may invariably make the 'happy', 'successful' performance of the corresponding illocutionary acts of warning depend on 'uptake'. But why suppose Austin is correct, and that this holds for all verbs whose inclusion in sentences makes them illocution-apt (i.e. enabling their speakers to perform illocutionary acts when uttering them in context)?

Different answers to these various questions permit a good number of distinct permutations of the 'uptake' claim. Which particular permutation, if any, was Austin endorsing? Commentators have tended to follow P. F. Strawson's lead here.[8] This is perfectly appropriate: Strawson's acquaintance with Austin gives

[7] See Gordon Baker and Peter Hacker *Language, Sense and Nonsense* (Oxford: Blackwell, 1984) pp. 69–76.

[8] P. F. Strawson 'Intention and convention in speech acts', reprinted in his *Logico-Linguistic Papers* (London: Methuen, 1971) pp. 149–69. See Mats Furberg 'Meaning and illocutionary force' in K. T. Fann ed. *Symposium on J. L. Austin* (London: Routledge and

him particular authority as an interpreter. Strawson ascribes the 'uptake' claim to Austin under its strongest interpretation.

On this interpretation (we can state it by answering each of our questions in turn) (i) No illocutionary act is performed without achievement of the specified effect; it is 'essential' to that performance.[9] (ii) The specified effect must always be on the 'intended' audience, the audience 'addressed'.[10] (iii) All illocutionary acts depend on achieving the specified effect, and this effect is always a matter of securing 'uptake', i.e. understanding the meaning and force of the locution.[11] (iv) Understanding the force of a locution is a matter of understanding a feature of the actual use of a sentence on a particular occasion, features which are to be identified and distinguished by the distinct meaning of whichever speech act verb is being used.[12] (v) 'Uptake' must be achieved by the speaker's knowing and intentional involvement.[13] (vi) The 'uptake' claim holds straightforwardly for all other cases as it does for warning; no general principle is required to underpin it.[14]

(We may wonder whether this is indeed what Austin intended. The interpretation essentially cancels the apparent guardedness in his phrasing. He could – and, to avoid misleading, should – simply have omitted 'happily, successfully' and 'generally' from his formulation of the 'uptake' claim. But we may set these concerns to one side, for the purposes of this chapter.)

What hangs on the 'uptake' claim? Its interest for Austin seems to be exhausted by the fact that it is one of three ways in which 'illocutionary acts are bound up with effects'.[15] This makes it a minor obstacle, easily overcome, on the path to distinguishing the illocutionary from the perlocutionary. So Austin did not stop to take note of what might otherwise seem quite a striking

---

Kegan Paul, 1969) pp. 445–67; p. 446; L. Jonathan Cohen 'Do illocutionary forces exist?' in *Symposium on J. L. Austin* pp. 420–44; p. 434.

[9] 'Intention and convention' p. 158.

[10] 'Intention and convention' p. 150. Strawson uses the phrases interchangeably in glossing Austin.

[11] 'Intention and convention' p. 158.

[12] Following Austin *How To Do Things With Words* pp. 148–50.

[13] 'Intention and convention' pp. 158–63. It is because Strawson assumed this was Austin's view that he was able to weld Austin's account of illocutionary acts to Grice's account of non-natural meaning.

[14] 'Intention and convention' p. 158. It is because Strawson assumed this was Austin's view that he objected to the 'uptake' claim in the way he did: by appeal to other cases in which it seemed equally straightforwardly *not* to hold.

[15] *How To Do Things With Words* p. 118. The others are 'taking effect' (e.g. in naming a ship *NN*, it is so named), and 'inviting a response', a matter of convention.

implication for his account of speech acts: that no privilege or authority attaches to speakers in determining whether or not illocutionary actions have been performed successfully.

P. F. Strawson first turned the 'uptake' claim to good effect, spotting a complementary deficiency in Austin and Grice.[16] Austin needs an analysis of the notion of audience understanding for his account of speech acts; his appeal to 'uptake' is merely a recognition of that gap, insufficient to fill it. Grice needs an extra condition to supplement his analysis of non-natural meaning; to mean something in this sense, the speaker must intend his audience to recognize his intention to produce a certain response by saying what he does. Strawson showed that, just as Austin's work on 'uptake' helps clarify the need for this condition, so Grice's work on intention helps provide an analysis of audience understanding.

More recently, philosophers have made the 'uptake' claim a crucial premise in arguments in political philosophy.[17] Suppose there are situations of a type, S, which systematically prevent an audience recognizing the illocutionary force, F, with which particular sorts of utterance, U, are issued in particular kinds of context, C. Given the 'uptake' claim, on the strong interpretation ascribed to Austin, the one uttering in such situations is rendered incapable of performing the speech acts they wish to perform. Hence there is reason to describe them as 'silenced' and to worry that their freedom of speech has been violated. In the canonical instance of this protest, situations of type S are generated or sustained by the publication and distribution of pornography, the kinds of context C are those in which women respond to male invitations to engage in sexual activity, the utterance of type U is 'No' or 'I do not want this' or their equivalents, and the illocutionary force F is that of refusal. But it is not difficult to conceive of other values for the symbols, and hence other applications for the same basic schema. Racism or homophobia, for example, may

---

[16] 'Intention and convention' sections III–IV.
[17] See in particular Rae Langton 'Speech acts and unspeakable acts' *Philosophy and Public Affairs* 22 (1993) pp. 305–30; Jennifer Hornsby 'Speech acts and pornography' in Susan Dwyer ed. *The Problem of Pornography* (California: Wadsworth, 1995) pp. 220–32; Rae Langton and Jennifer Hornsby 'Free speech and illocution' *Legal Theory* 4 (1998) pp. 21–37. For a careful overview, see Miranda Fricker *Epistemic Injustice* (Oxford: Oxford University Press, 2007) pp. 137–42.

be equally responsible for generating and sustaining situations of type S, and hence, perhaps, equally liable to 'silence' people and violate free speech.

Views such as these depend on the 'uptake' claim in its strongest form, as attributed to Austin. Weaker variants are not sufficient. As we shall see, for example, some think that what is required for the successful performance of an illocutionary act is not that speakers *achieve* the 'uptake' of their audience, but either that they *aim* to secure it, or that they *reasonably expect* to secure it. Both variants fall far short of what the 'silencing' argument requires. For example, a woman in the canonical situation could utter 'No', fail to be understood as refusing by her audience, and yet succeed in the illocutionary act she attempts. It is enough that she aimed to be understood as refusing, or that she reasonably expected to be so understood.[18] Since the woman's attempt at an illocutionary act succeeds, she is not 'silenced'; the situation has not deprived her of her capacity to act in the way she has tried to act.

II

So much for what the 'uptake' claim means and implies. Is it true? Several speech act theorists have endorsed the claim.[19] But there are good reasons to pursue the issue. Partly because a good number of speech act theorists have rejected it explicitly.[20] Partly because some theorists seem to reject it implicitly, placing no such requirement on purportedly exhaustive lists of necessary conditions for illocutionary acts.[21] Partly because Austin, as we

---

[18] Proponents are willing to grant both: even if the woman knows her response probably will not secure 'uptake', given the situation created by the production and distribution of pornography, it is not she who is to be held at fault – precisely because she has aimed to be understood as refusing and because she reasonably expects to be so understood.

[19] See G. J. Warnock *J. L. Austin* (London: Routledge, 1989) p. 127; L. W. Forgoson 'Locutionary and illocutionary acts' in Isaiah Berlin et al *Essays on J. L. Austin* (Oxford: Oxford University Press, 1973) pp. 160–85; pp. 169–70; Keith Graham *J. L. Austin* (Sussex: Harvester Press, 1977) p. 91.

[20] See William P. Alston *Illocutionary Acts and Sentence Meaning* (Ithaca: Cornell University Press, 2000) pp. 24; 67; Daniel Jacobson 'Freedom of speech acts? A response to Langton' *Philosophy and Public Affairs* 24 (1995) pp. 64–79; Alexander Bird 'Illocutionary silencing' *Pacific Philosophical Quarterly* 83 (2002) pp. 1–15.

[21] See John Searle *Speech Acts: An essay in the Philosophy of Language* (Cambridge: Cambridge University Press, 1969; John Searle and Daniel Vanderveken *Foundations of Illocu-*

128 MAXIMILIAN DE GAYNESFORD

have seen, employed language ('not . . . happily, successfully performed') that allowed himself a clear get-out on the issue. But mainly because all parties to the dispute are missing the point. The issue is not set up in such a way as to allow for fruitful debate.

We might have anticipated this. Participants in the debate have tended to think that the claim is either just obviously true for all illocutionary acts, or just obviously false of any of them, that there is no need to provide argument or detailed response to counterclaims, and that it is sufficient instead merely to point to particular cases of illocutionary acts. Moreover, participants only ever point to a tiny sample of cases, and they appeal to different samples, depending on which side they support.[22]

Austin set the pattern at the beginning of debate, arguing in favour of the 'uptake' claim by appeal to the case of warning alone. At the other end of the spectrum, the most recent contribution to debate, by an opponent of the claim, appeals to the cases of asking and telling alone:

> Whether I told you that the dean is coming to dinner or asked you to bring me a towel does not hang on whether you heard or understood me. If you didn't, my communicative purpose has been frustrated. But it doesn't follow that I didn't tell you or ask you.[23]

But would this speaker – *could* he – remain so blithe in the face of your non-comprehension had he been attempting to *warn* you that the dean is coming to dinner? (This is a fair question, since Alston believes that illocutionary acts *never* depend on 'uptake' for their successful performance.) There would, surely, be something bizarre about my continuing to insist 'Well, I did *warn* you!' once I know you have either not heard or not understood me. The natural move to make, on learning that this is how things stand, is to retreat a step: 'Well I did *try* to warn you'. And the most

tionary Logic (Cambridge: Cambridge University Press, 1985); Daniel Vanderveken *Meaning and Speech Acts* vols I–II (Cambridge: Cambridge University Press, 1990, 1991).

[22] This holds for those who support the claim (e.g. Geoffrey Warnock, L. W. Forgoson, Keith Graham, Rae Langton and Jennifer Hornsby) and for those who reject it (e.g. William Alston, Alexander Bird and Daniel Jacobson).

[23] William Alston *Illocutionary Acts* p. 24.

plausible explanation for what makes this retreat natural is the ready admission that, not having secured your understanding, I have not actually warned you.[24]

Even those inclined to be cautious and careful have depended on a minute sample of cases. P. F. Strawson, for example, never goes further than to say that he is 'tempted' to reject the 'uptake' claim. On the one hand, he is clearly impressed by Austin's appeal to warning.[25] On the other hand, he is worried by objections – attributed to H. L. A. Hart – which again consider only a tiny range of cases: 'surely a man may . . . actually have made such and such a bequest, or gift, even if no one ever reads his will or instrument of gift'.[26] Mentioning no other instances than these, Strawson is nevertheless prepared to commit himself to an equally general, though more modest position: the successful performance of illocutionary acts requires that the speaker at least have the *aim* of achieving the 'uptake' of the intended audience.[27] L. Jonathan Cohen, equally careful, but moved by no greater a range of cases, thinks we can be sure of a position that is somewhat stronger. Aim is not enough; the speaker's utterance must be 'of a kind that he could reasonably expect to secure uptake'.[28]

So the first task is to acquaint ourselves with a range of cases. The materials are to hand. Parties at either end of the spectrum on the 'uptake' claim (Austin, Alston), together with those who may be uncommitted (Searle and Vanderveken), have all provided extensive lists of verbs exemplifying their classifications of illocutionary acts.[29] Drawing only from what is common to these various pools, we can assemble the following sentences; in uttering each, on some occasion of use, a speaker attempts to perform the very illocutionary act named in the sentence:

1. 'I concede the victory in this campaign to you'.
2. 'I describe myself as a federalist'.
3. 'I bet you £5 that the economy will now improve'.

---

[24] The OED gives an even stronger profile to 'warn' in its primary sense: 'to make aware, to put on guard'.
[25] 'Intention and convention' p. 150.
[26] 'Intention and convention' p. 158.
[27] 'Intention and convention' p. 158.
[28] 'Do illocutionary forces exist?' p. 435.
[29] Austin *How To Do Things With Words* pp. 148–63; Alston *Illocutionary Acts* pp. 81–143; Searle and Vanderveken *Foundations of Illocutionary Logic* 179–216.

4. 'I accept that I was mistaken'.
5. 'I entreat you to apply for the job'.
6. 'I consent to leave'.
7. 'I adjourn this meeting'.
8. 'I curse this place and all who live in it'.
9. 'I thank you for your gift'.
10. 'I blame you for this mess'.

Each of these sentences may be distinguished in various ways from each of the others. But on the present issue, the 'uptake' claim, they seem to divide into two groups only: those which name acts that are vulnerable to 'uptake' failure and those which name acts that are immune to such failure.

To determine which group a sentence falls into, we need only imagine ourselves in the position of the speaker of that sentence on some occasion of its use, and ask a diagnostic question. Where the variable f takes illocutionary force indicators as its values, p takes sentences expressing propositions, and 'utter' ranges over all means of producing linguistic tokens, the question has this form: 'I uttered "$f(p)$" with the intention of performing thereby the illocutionary act of type f, but *did* I thereby perform an illocutionary act of that type?'

It would be perfectly reasonable to ask this question in relation to each of the odd-numbered sentences, and sometimes advisable to obtain an answer. One might intelligibly think to oneself, for example, 'I did *say* "I thank you for your gift", with the intention of thereby thanking my mother, but I wonder whether I actually *thanked* her, for it seems that she did not hear me, or if she did hear me that she did not understand my words, or if she did understand my words that she nevertheless, and for whatever reason, did not grasp that I was *thanking* her'. Sentences of this sort we may regard as 'uptake-dependent' in the sense that those who use them are vulnerable to a particular kind of failure: although there is indeed an utterance of the relevant sentence $f(p)$ in a particular context i, and although the one uttering it, S, intends to issue it with the illocutionary force f named in the utterance, and thus to perform the relevant illocutionary action A, S may nevertheless fail to perform A because, and only because, the audience H to whom he directs the utterance, and to whom he intends to direct it, though present in context i and able to understand what S says, nevertheless fails to recognize it as having force f.

Contrast these cases with the even-numbered sentences. If it is ever reasonable to ask our diagnostic question of these, that is not because such utterances might lack an audience that understands their force. If I say 'I describe myself as a federalist', for example, and somehow fail to perform the illocutionary act of describing something, that could not be because no audience recognized the utterance as an attempt to describe something. I need no audience to describe myself, let alone one that understands my utterance as having descriptive force. The same goes for utterances in which I accept, consent, curse or blame. Sentences of this sort we may regard as 'uptake-free' in the sense that those who use them are, in doing so, immune to the particular kind of failure defined above.

Three features of these categories, the 'uptake-dependent' and the 'uptake-free', are worth noting. First, it seems that neither category is peculiar to any particular sort of illocutionary act. For examples of each category may be found in each of the usual ways of classifying such acts. We can demonstrate this with our ten cases:

Class of Illocutionary Act	**'Uptake-Dependent'**	**'Uptake Free'**
Expositives (Assertives)	Concede	Describe
Commissives	Bet	Accept
Directives	Entreat	Consent
Exercitives (Declaratives)	Adjourn	Curse
Behabitives (Expressives)	Thank	Blame

Second, the two categories distinguish illocutionary acts according to their illocutionary performance conditions, not their intended perlocutionary effects. It is because the audience needs to *recognize* that it is warned that 'I warn you not to come closer' is 'uptake-dependent', not because the audience needs to *heed* that warning.

Finally, the two categories are not restricted to the explicit performative type (as in our examples). They also subdivide utterances whose illocutionary force is implicit. When I say 'Don't tread on that snake', for example, intending to perform the illocutionary act of warning, that act is 'uptake-dependent'. When I say 'I am a federalist', intending to perform the illocutionary act of describing, that act is 'uptake-free'.

It would be premature to expect acceptance of all that has been said. There may be some, even considerable, disagreement about

how to categorize the individual sentences, distinguishing
between those whose utterance tends to effect illocutionary acts
that are 'uptake-dependent' and those which do not. Much here
requires argument and, perhaps, adjustment. But if the rough
picture of a distinction between the 'uptake-dependent' and
the 'uptake-free' seems correct, we can see why debate about
the 'uptake' claim has foundered. Neither side could be right,
for the debate rests on a mistake: that it could intelligibly be a
disagreement about the notion of the illocutionary act *simpliciter*.
The question of 'uptake' does not arise at this higher level, the
genus 'illocutionary act'. It arises only at the subsidiary level,
concerning species of that genus. Some sentences are used in
utterances to effect acts that are 'uptake-dependent', some to
effect acts that are 'uptake-free'. We may argue about which sentences belong in which set, but it makes no sense to ask of 'the
illocutionary act' whether *it* belongs in either set. It was Austin
who set debate on its impossible course, assuming we might intelligibly assert or deny that 'the performance of *an illocutionary act*
involves the securing of uptake'.[30]

More can be said if the rough picture seems correct. The
'silencing' argument turns on whether 'the illocutionary act' is
performed in circumstances where no 'uptake' is forthcoming. So
debate on this issue is also confused, and for the same reason. The
issue cannot be decided by appeal to the notion of 'the illocutionary act' *simpliciter*. But this is not the only difficulty. Suppose
debate were made responsive to the fact that only some illocutionary acts are 'uptake-dependent'. The issue then becomes whether
the speaker who utters a sentence, and thus attempts to perform
an illocutionary act of some sort, is attempting to perform an act
of a sort that is uptake-dependent.

This seems highly implausible in the canonical instance of the
'silencing' argument, where women say 'No' in an attempt to
perform the illocutionary act of refusing. For acts of this sort are
surely immune to audience 'uptake' failure in the specific and
relevant sense. There may be many ways I might fail to perform
the illocutionary act of refusing: by not intending to refuse; by
accepting instead; by saying nothing in a situation where silence
means consent; by saying something ('Rule Britannia') in a situation where it could not mean refusal; and so on. But one way

[30] *How To Do Things With Words* p. 117; my emphasis.

I cannot fail is because the audience does not recognize the utterance as having the force of refusal. As immigrants know to their cost, a suitably deputed official can successfully refuse them permission to enter the country by uttering a formula to that effect, and this act is successfully performed even if the immigrant does not speak the official's language and hence fails to understand what the formula means, let alone what force it has. The same may hold in the canonical instance. The audience of the woman's 'No' may be sufficiently affected by pornography that he is unable to recognize her utterance as having the force of refusal. But if refusal is 'uptake-free', the woman succeeds in performing the act she attempted to perform. Then pornography would not have 'silenced' her or violated her freedom of speech.

This need not be the end of the matter, however. Once we are suitably responsive to the distinction between 'uptake-free' and 'uptake-dependent' acts, it should be possible to repair the gap left by the loss of refusal to the 'uptake-free' category. Suppose that the production and distribution of pornography prevents audiences from recognizing the force of a speaker's utterances when she attempts to advise, or alert, or caution, or inform, or retract, or veto, or warn. The successful performance of such acts is patently 'uptake-dependent'. So we might use these results to construct various scenarios in which the speaker is properly described as 'silenced' by pornography, and where the overall situation is one in which pornography violates free speech.

III

It seems perfectly clear that Austin's doctrine of the 'uptake-dependency' of the illocutionary act does not hold generally. Some illocutionary acts are 'uptake-dependent'; others are not. But recognition that this is so immediately raises a question: why is it that illocutionary acts divide in this way? At issue are the relevant features which make the utterance of some verbal forms give rise to 'uptake-dependent' acts and some give rise to 'uptake-free' acts. The answer may be complex, and what follows is only a start at dealing with this question. But there are three plausible areas in which we might look for the relevant features. What is distinctive may be a matter of (i) the kinds of content which may or may not be appended to the relevant verbal forms; (ii) the modes of directedness which may or may not be associated with the verbal forms; or (iii) the essential characteristics of those to whom utterances with the relevant verbal forms may or may not be directed.

There were five verbal forms noted above whose utterance gives rise to 'uptake-dependent' illocutionary acts – 'uptake-dependent' forms, for short. One striking feature common to several of these is what we might call their 'content hunger'. I cannot just concede, bet, or entreat: the concession, bet and entreaty must have content. I concede to you that . . . , I bet you that . . . , I entreat you to. . . . (The speaker need not express that content, of course; it may be understood, given previous remarks, or left implicit.) The contrast is with verbal forms like 'acquit', 'demote' and 'excommunicate' which need not have content in the sense described. Now several of these contrastive verbal forms are to be found amongst 'uptake-independent' forms. Thus I can simply describe you, accept you, and curse you.

This may give hope of explaining the 'uptake-dependent' / 'uptake-free' division in terms of what is and what is not content-hungry. The idea seems plausible enough: those which are hungry in this way can only be satisfied when certain requirements are met, and one of those requirements may be that the audience grasp what those contents are. But this cannot be the explanation we are looking for. This is partly because some 'uptake-independent' forms are also 'content hungry'. I cannot simply consent; there must be something, for example, that I consent to do (for you). Similarly, I cannot simply blame you; there must be something I blame you for. It is also partly because some 'uptake-dependent' forms need have no such content. I can simply adjourn a meeting, for example. ('Thank' is an awkward case: it seems right on most occasions, but not all perhaps, to insist that if I thank you, there must be something I thank you for.) These points generalize when we look beyond the ten verbal forms specified above.

A second striking feature, shared by all five 'uptake-dependent' forms we have looked at, is what we might call their directedness. I cannot just concede, bet, entreat, adjourn, or thank in a vacuum. There must be someone to whom I concede, someone with whom I make the bet, someone whom I entreat, some meeting which I adjourn, some person or persons whom I thank. (Again, speakers may assume or leave implicit which persons or things are the objects of this directedness.) The issues here quickly become quite complex. For example, we should distinguish between existence and identity, between verbal forms with a directedness that requires simply that a person or thing exist, and forms whose directedness requires that some particular person or thing exist. But the main contrast is with verbal forms which lack the need for either form of directedness. Thus I can lament, acknowledge, predict and guess without there being any person or thing to whom, or with whom, I do these things. And several of these contrastive verbal forms can be found amongst 'uptake-independent' forms. Thus I can describe, accept and consent without there being any person or thing to whom, or with whom, I do these things.

So the hope arises of explaining the 'uptake-dependent' / 'uptake-free' division in terms of what is and what is not 'directed' in the sense described. Again, the idea seems plausible enough: those which are 'directed' in this way may have special conditions attached to them, such that the successful performance of the relevant illocutionary acts require that an audience grasp how they are directed. But, again, this cannot be the explanation we are looking for. For some 'uptake-independent' forms are also 'directed'. Thus I cannot simply curse or blame; there must be some person or thing I curse or blame, some object to which these actions of mine are directed. Again, these points generalize when we look beyond the ten verbal forms specified above.

The five 'uptake-dependent' forms share a third striking feature. All five must be directed at a person or thing, as we know. But it is not enough that the verbal form be directed in this way. There are two particular ways in which this insufficiency manifests itself. To perform actions using some verbal forms, the utterance must be addressed to the person or thing to whom they are directed. To perform actions using some verbal forms, the utterance must be witnessed, or there must be evidence supplying for the absence of a witness. We can take each in turn, using examples.

Some utterances must be addressed to the person or thing to whom they are directed. I cannot simply bet someone, entreat someone or thank someone. To count as a betting, an entreating, a thanking, my utterance must be addressed (explicitly or implicitly) to the relevant person. Contrast this with cursing, blaming, conceding and adjourning. To be engaged in these actions is to be directed towards some person or thing, but not necessarily to address them. I can adjourn the meeting though I am addressing you; I can blame you though I am addressing your superior; I can curse your superior though I am addressing the gods. These examples should put paid to the idea that we might explain the 'uptake-dependent' / 'uptake-free' division in terms of the 'address' requirement alone. It is true that none of the 'uptake-free' forms are dependent in this way. Either they need not be directed in the first place (describe, accept, consent), or their directedness need not be associated with this mode of address (curse, blame). But some of the 'uptake-dependent' forms are not dependent in this way either (concede, adjourn).

Some utterances must be witnessed or there must be evidence supplying for the absence of a witness. I cannot concede to someone, bet someone or adjourn something without either someone being present who observes these things and is in a position to testify to their having occurred, or there being some evidence (e.g. a written note) that they have occurred. (The witnesses need not be wholly passive observers, of course; they may be participants in the activity.) Contrast this with cursing, blaming, entreating and thanking. To be engaged in these actions is to be directed towards some person or thing, but not necessarily to require witnesses or evidence. I can curse or blame you though I am alone; I can 'thank or entreat you though there are no witnesses to the event and no evidence that it has occurred. It is tempting to try to explain the 'uptake-dependent' / 'uptake-free' division in terms of the 'witness' requirement alone: those illocutionary acts which are 'witness-dependent' may have special conditions attached to them, such that their successful performance requires that the witness grasp what he has witnessed. But our examples undermine this possibility also. It is true that none of the 'uptake-free' forms are 'witness-dependent'. Either they need not be directed in the first place (describe, accept, consent), or their directedness need not be associated with the act of witnessing (curse, blame). But some of the 'uptake-dependent' forms are not 'witness-dependent' either (entreat, thank).

We need not be disheartened. Our evidence is consistent with a disjunctive explanation. If the verbal forms are *either* address- or witness-dependent, then they are 'uptake-dependent':

	Content Hungry	Directed	Address-Dependent	Witness-Dependent
Concede	Yes	Yes	No	Yes
Bet	Yes	Yes	Yes	Yes
Entreat	Yes	Yes	Yes	No
Adjourn	No	Yes	No	Yes
Thank	No	Yes	Yes	No

And if the verbal forms are *neither* address- nor witness-dependent, they are 'uptake-free':

	Content Hungry	Directed	Address-Dependent	Witness-Dependent
Describe	No	No	No	No
Accept	No	No	No	No
Consent	Yes	No	No	No
Curse	No	Yes	No	No
Blame	Yes	Yes	No	No

So these might be the relevant features which make forms either 'uptake-dependent' or 'uptake-free'.

To summarize this attempt at an explanation for our earlier findings, it seems that illocutionary acts fall into two categories: those which require 'uptake' if they are to be successfully performed and those which do not. The former fall into two subcategories: the address-dependent and the witness-dependent. And these features may be connected: it is because only some types of illocutionary act require an addressee or a witness that only some are 'uptake-dependent'.

INDEX

Agents and Their Actions, First Edition. Edited by Maximilian de Gaynesford. © 2011 Blackwell
Publishing Ltd. Published 2011 by Blackwell Publishing Ltd.